READ, REFLECT, RESPOND
The 3 Rs of Growth and Change

Gloria Vanderhorst, PhD

www.TotalPublishingAndMedia.com

Copyright © 2024 Gloria Vanderhorst, PhD

All rights reserved.

No part of this book may be reproduced, stored in a retrieval system, or transmitted by any means, electronic, mechanical, photocopying, recording, or otherwise, without written permission from the author.

ISBN: 978-1-63302-303-1

Table of Contents

Welcome: Introduction to Your Guided Journal. v

Meet Gloria vii

Organization of the Book 1

    Section 1: Planning Your Life 2

    Section 2: Identifying Obstacles 12

    Section 3: Connecting with Others 22

    Section 4: Working with Others 34

    Section 5: Maintaining Connections 44

    Section 6: Obstacles to Connecting 54

    Section 7: Connecting with Family 64

    Section 8: Fostering Physical Wellbeing 76

    Section 9: Understanding Change and Growth 86

    Section 10: Evaluation – A Bonus Essay! 106

Comments from Readers 108

Welcome: Introduction to Your Guided Journal.

You may already be a fan of Dr. V and Me. If so, then welcome to your private journal that will guide you through the next year and support you in growing in the process of self-exploration. If you are new and exploring ways to better understand yourself and challenge yourself to grow emotionally, then you are in the right place.

This book will provide you with 52 weeks to deeply connect with REFLECTING on your relationships, and the life you want to live. Join me in your journey of exploration. Read, reflect, and respond. Engage your mind in exploring your past as it clearly shapes the future. Learn how your experiences have impacted your thoughts and feelings. Explore the myriad influences on your life. Grow as you reflect and challenge yourself to look deeper into your history. Address the future in ways that will benefit you and those you love. Enjoy the journey.

Each week, you will be challenged to read one essay and take a few moments to reflect on what you have read. You will notice that the response page has three questions. Choose one of these for your focus or generate a question of your own. The response page is not lined; the lines are missing on purpose. Your earliest memories are stored in images, sounds, and experiences of touch. To access those your brain will need to draw, scribble, scratch, and create. Let your brain guide your responses. At the end of the year, you will know yourself better.

At the end of the year, you will have gained insights, expanded your world, and committed to connecting with yourself and others in a new way.

Enjoy! Grow!

Meet Gloria

This book has been a pleasure to create. My intent was to make each entry unique, enabling you to engage yourself in historical facts and present experiences while finding humor and deep meaning in your history. I want to lead you to reflect on the history that has shaped you to date and to explore the present influences that impact you today. With that wisdom, you can choose how to move forward and make meaningful choices for the future.

For me, personal stories are the basis of relationships, both with others and with ourselves. We are born connected to another person, and we spend the rest of our lives seeking connections with others. This engagement, whether positive or negative, shapes us and molds our interests, personalities, and day-to-day functioning. As you reflect on your personal stories, you will be drawn to see patterns and nuances that will lead you to try new things and discard old things. Be willing to do both with respect.

My career as a psychologist has covered the lifespan, from working with preschool children to tweens and teens then on to adults and the aging population. I have seen human development and interactions across the lifespan. The landscape of life is rich and fascinating.

I hope that these entries help you to discover riches in your own life, and stir you to be intentional with your own emotional growth. We are dynamic creatures, ever changing whether we recognize it or not. Use these entries wisely.

Organization of the Book

This book is divided into ten sections, as noted in the index. Each section brings together pieces of our lives. Altogether there are fifty-two entries to correspond with the 52 weeks of the year; however, life is not orderly. Therefore, you do not have to move through the entries in sequence, nor are they numbered in sequence. Each section has its own numbering. Feel free to bounce around, or if you prefer to move in order, enjoy. The entries are to be contemplated over the course of a week. You may address each entry more than once over the course of the week, or you may address an entry just once. The choice is yours. In my view, the repetition will help you go deeper.

Journals are intended to be used on a regular basis and in private reflection. You may want to find a routine time each week to read and reflect. I would suggest that you set aside 40 to 60 minutes for maximum benefit. Reflection takes time. Self-exploration is a serious endeavor that will reward you with understanding, meaning, and strengthening. Your brain has a marvelous storage capacity. Unbelievably, that organ has recorded every experience that you have ever had and still has the capacity to store more than you can ever imagine. Take time to give it space to recall pieces of history that have been important influences on you. You may be surprised at how your past experiences have been influencing your present.

Unlike other journals that you may have used, this one has blank pages for reflection. This is intentional. Our brain stores experiences in verbal and nonverbal ways. Accessing each of these is important. Give yourself permission and opportunity to access the non-verbal reactions to each entry, as well as the verbal ones. Three stimulating phrases or questions are provided as prompts with each entry. You may use these as starting points, or you may skip past them. Trust yourself to choose how to proceed. Allowing the pen, pencil, or crayon to move around the page and draw out parts of your history that are stored in terms of experience, reaction, and other non-verbal forms is an important part of self-exploration.

You may also wish to return to this journal years later. Guided journals are important in this way. We can see how we have changed and grown. We can be reminded of issues that we have set aside and need to revisit. We can reflect on how we have been challenged and responded. We can swell with pride as we see our maturity, and revel in how well we have accepted challenges.

SECTION 1

PLANNING YOUR LIFE

1. HIGH PRIORITY

I must admit the phrase "High Priority" is tossed about frequently. "Oh yes, ma'am! You are a high priority, and we will fix your refrigerator as soon as the part arrives", or "Oh yes, sir, your order is a high priority for us. We are tracking it daily and will keep you posted". REALLY! You can tell we have had some repair needs recently. But what does "High Priority" really mean?

Doesn't "priority" mean the right to take precedence over all others? Doesn't it mean the right to go first? How could something be higher than that? Are you kidding me? You might guess that the recent service needed in this house is related to the refrigerator dying two days before the family holiday celebration!

However, having priorities is essential. A friend of mine recently reminded me of this in a big way. To start the new year, she had a beautiful bracelet made with one word: "priority." Each day, as she puts on her jewelry, that bracelet catches her eye and causes her to pause to look at the day ahead. She decides what the priority of the day will be. What a marvelous idea! Start your day by **choosing** what will take precedence. Each day is thoughtful. At the same time, anything goes. Today, I might float on a raft in the pool, complete a chapter in my book, organize my taxes, or restock the now-working refrigerator. The point is I get to choose! I can be thoughtful.

Of course, our days have those "musts" in them. You have a new baby, and you must do the responsible things, so the baby is fed, soothed, and loved. You have work obligations that need your attention. You have groceries to fetch. At the same time, you can choose to prioritize. Your day will go better if you take 15 minutes to read the thought for the day and focus your attention for a few minutes before starting the "have tos." You can look forward to the one time you will invest in something you enjoy or a project you have been putting off. I want to propose that there is no such thing as a "high" priority. If it is a priority, then nothing tops it. Nothing is higher. Let us get the English language straight. Priority means first, top, and most important. Nothing is higher.

Unbundle! Do the radical thing of making the English language meaningful. I challenge you to put one word in front of you each morning. It does not have to be a "priority." It does not have to be a beautiful bracelet. It can be a sticky note on the bathroom mirror. For you, it may be "think," "focus," or "pray." Choose one word meaningful for you. Right before the holiday, mine would have been "refrigerator"!!

REFLECTING

1. Imagine that you have a "priority" bracelet. choose a priority word for the day.
2. Record why you chose it.
3. How did you use it throughout the day/week?

2. THE FED HAS RAISED INTEREST RATES

From time to time, the Federal Reserve decides to raise interest rates to stave off rising inflation. The process goes like this: when prices are climbing, a rise in interest rates makes buying those things more difficult. The idea is that, as buying goes down, the producers of things will lower prices, causing more people to buy them.

The economy's ebb and flow depend on this balance. The Fed is trying to find that sweet spot where manufacturers can make a decent living, consumers can afford new gadgets, and both parties can be content with the flow of money. How is this balance kept? How is it helpful? Balance in the economy is essential and critical. The same is true for our lives. Balance is life-giving. When the economy is balanced, people can afford food, clothing, and luxuries within limits. People can feel their earned income is helping them to live a good life and not just helping them to get by.

When we are out of balance, we are in trouble. We are at risk of falling. Who or what will be there to catch us? The Federal Reserve trusts that, when they raise interest rates, there will be a corrective response, and prices will adjust and come down. Consumers will start buying again, then interest rates can decrease, and the merry-go-round continues. This cooperative process can work very well for the individual and the economy. This is all about balance.

How do you put balance into your life? What would we see if we were to do a factual report of your time for the past week? Lay out a timeline on the page. Where did you go? What did you do? What did you experience? What drew your attention? What did you accomplish? How we invest our time can give us precise information about our priorities. Often, we do not "invest" our time. Instead, we let time and demands carry us along like a current, and we do not make decisions or set priorities. When we do this, we do ourselves and our families a disservice. Our time is precious, and we must treat it as an investment and decide how we spend our time.

You say you love your family, and your calendar shows you never made it home for dinner in the past week. You missed your daughter's swim meet for a client call. You value your physical health, yet the treadmill in the basement is a place to hang coats. You fancy yourself an intellectual, but have not read a book in the past six months, and you fall asleep in front of the television every night. You love your spouse, but have not "made love" in a long time. Need I go on?

How would you rate your interest in you? Your family? Your spouse? Your children? Your health? Your intellect? Scrutinize these. It is time to raise your interest rates. Now is the time to make decisions, and invest in what you value.

REFLECTING

1. Quickly list your priorities (family, friends, work, exercise, entertainment, social, political, religious, physical, etc.) and now track your time for each during the week.
2. Now that you have a real record to review. How does the recorded time fit with your stated priorities? What changes do you need to make?

3. WHAT IS SPRING?

Spring is a glorious season on the United States' East Coast. Here in the Nation's Capital, we anticipate and enjoy the hundreds of Cherry Trees planted along the Tidal Basin. People come from miles away to experience the blossoms. Cameras are clicking away, brides are posing under the luscious pink blossoms, and children pick petals off the ground. Spring is a glorious time of renewal and hope. The anticipation is exciting. The blossoms are a perfect light pink, and the carpet of petals they leave is elegant.

Even if you cannot see a blooming cherry tree in your yard, the season is intended to spark your imagination – leading to new plans. What are you planning? Some of my clients are planning weddings. That is exciting! Some of my clients are contemplating going back to school and changing careers. That is a challenge, and I admire their bravery. Your brain must do things it has not done in a long while. Studying is a whole different form of work, and sometimes, the old anxieties from earlier schooling can return with a vengeance.

I admire these new students. We all have memories of school as children. Whether we liked it or not, these old memories are bound to appear when we put ourselves back into the classroom or any learning environment. Actually, you are doing that right now as you work through these essays! Were you the class clown or the head of the class? Were you lost in some classes and comfortable in others? Was studying fun for you or the very thing that you dreaded? We spend 12 to 16 years in a classroom. That is a sizable chunk of time. When we choose to return as adults, that history will come back to life. You are not only enrolling in classes as an adult, but revisiting classroom experiences from that 12-to16-year period. Here is the place for the Scout motto: Be Prepared.

As you work through these essays and the accompanying questions, some part of you will be drawn back into previous learning situations.

Preparing to return to learning as an adult is more than buying the text or saving time to be on Zoom. Preparing for your earlier history to jump out when you least expect it would be best. So, let us get ahead of this. Take time to review your earlier history of being in school. I mean, go as far back as you can. Remember being dropped off at preschool? Remember the best friend in elementary school who dropped you with the transition to middle school? Were you a successful student, or did you face challenges?

Trust me, all these pieces of history will come flooding or creeping into your current experience. Welcome them, as they will help you grow. Go fishing for them to take advantage of the feelings that come to mind. Spring into this new adventure with the awareness that your history can help or hurt you. Decide to use your history, rather than letting it overwhelm you.

REFLECTING

1. Page back to your earliest school memories. Express the feelings that come up.
2. How are these feelings challenging your ability to move forward on past or current plans?
3. With the "new" thing in front of you, how do you feel about the challenge to master the problematic thoughts, feelings, and old learning habits? What help will you seek?

4. WHAT IS YOUR MISSION?

Recently, I heard the head of a popular business talk about the motivation behind starting his business. The type of business does not matter here. What impressed me was his "reason" for starting a business. When I think of what motivates someone to start a business, I think of the financial gain or need. We are driven to survive, and sometimes, to do that, we need to be entrepreneurs. But this guy did not need the money. He already had more than he and his family would need for a few generations – and could ever spend. What drove him to dive back into the day-to-day grind and pressure of starting and running a business was the desire to give back to our veterans and other groups who have contributed to our country and tend to be forgotten. He was passionate about honoring our veterans and helping others remember that this country was built on the sacrifice of human lives. That is such a humbling thought.

I met a woman who uses her voice to educate and influence others. She told the story of studying communication as an outlier in her class. Most of her peers considered going into media somehow and putting their voices into the newspaper, television, or advertising. Yet, she wanted to use her voice to influence and persuade. She wanted to speak to others. The thought was entirely novel. It is a very unusual space as most communication majors end up in print or on the television, reading from a teleprompter. She wanted to use her voice to educate and influence those at the top levels of their professions. She trained to deliver speeches that would persuade, motivate, challenge, and sometimes even shame. She wanted to influence in a variety of ways. The advisors around her tried to move her off this goal and tell her no one could make a living just speaking. Yet, I have just heard her do that very thing. She uses her voice to confront, persuade, and encourage others to make changes. She is a professional persuader! She has met her goal and loves what she does.

What do you want to do? How often have you let your mind wander into this territory? Do you have a dream and an image of how you will change the world? What is your "change the world" project? How will you turn this into reality?

Take this mind wandering and corral it. Permit yourself to seek support from those in your circle of influence. Let your mind wander into territories that have been taboo or scary in the past. You can move forward and explore new paths. Every product, every process, every invention started with an idea. What ideas are floating around in your brain? How are you treating these ideas? Do you brush them aside as silly or too hard? Take a day. Mark your calendar to take yourself seriously. Set aside time to imagine what and how you would do it. Just start.

REFLECTING

1. Do you have a mission?
2. What is your mission for the future?
3. What is your plan for executing this mission?
4. What is the first step you have taken? What did you learn?

5. KALEIDOSCOPE

Do you remember this marvelous toy? I remember receiving one of these for a birthday when I was ten and how fascinating this tube was. Of course, as a child, I got this cardboard tube filled at one end with colorful crystals you could hear rolling around as you turned the collar and viewed the changing color combinations through the other end. There are many assorted sizes of kaleidoscopes, and they were initially a part of the study of light. Then, they were made to give artists visual assistance in seeing color combinations and complexity. In many ways, the kaleidoscope could be a metaphor for life itself. A simple tube with infinite possibilities. Isn't that what life is?

We look from one perspective or angle, yet the reality is more complex, colorful, and changeable than we can imagine. Each of our worlds is complex. We have childhood histories, relationship histories, internal experiences, hopes, dreams, and challenges. Our world, internally and externally, is complex. Some of us embrace the complexity and dive into it as exciting or fascinating. Others get trapped in the bits and pieces of odd shapes and sharp corners. Where are you?

Life is complex—it has always been complex. Just think of the beginning of this story: You come into the world with no ability to feed yourself, clothe yourself, or communicate your needs. YIKES! That is some beginning. Interfacing with the world around us is necessary for survival. How we do that, especially in infancy, is enormously important. We are dependent creatures, and others become dependent on us as we grow. We are a collection of colorful pieces and parts that can be interesting, attractive, sharp, and blinding.

How are you approaching life? How are you experiencing the world around you? We make choices which influence how we experience the world every moment of the day. Take one day and pay close attention to your many options. Every second of the day, we are facing choices. The kaleidoscope is constantly turning. Think of the colored crystals falling in the kaleidoscope and how many combinations exist. Our lives have this same complexity. Yet, we tend to gravitate away from the complex to the more straightforward routine. We prefer calm to chaos. We prefer order to confusion. We prefer direction to free form. And at the same time, we remain fascinated by the colorful possibilities.

We have many choices as we move throughout the day, the week, the month, the year... you get it. Each choice will lead to another until the path is set in one direction. Once it is set, we often have difficulty turning the tube to create a new scene. We tend to get stuck and plow forward on paths that do not suit us well. It is too bad we cannot just shake the kaleidoscope and start over—or wait. We can. You have more options than you may think. The picture that you see can change. Just turn the collar on the tube.

REFLECTING

1. Describe your life as you currently see it.
2. Now, turn the corner and describe what you want your life to be.
3. What are the steps you need to take to get there?

SECTION 2

IDENTIFYING OBSTACLES

1. YOUR MENTAL STORAGE LOCKER

Did you know you have a storage locker? Storage lockers are places where we keep the "junk and stuff" about our lives and existence. Humans love to collect and save. Businesses like Self Storage, and Extra Space Storage, and hundreds across the country make a living out of holding our junk and stuff and charging us for doing so! The attic is full, or the storage locker in our apartment building is overflowing. We need help deciding which stuff to junk, so we rent a storage locker.

On some level, we know we will never go through this stuff. Our children will be left with that responsibility. I know some families where the children have been methodical in going through the self-storage locker and others where they have just called "College Hunks Hauling Junk" and let everything go. Of course, when you do that, you may miss the 3-carat diamond ring Mom stashed in the back of the secretary.

There is no right or wrong to this process. Even though we tell ourselves to save this stuff for the next generation, we save it for ourselves. Deciding to let go of great grandpa's razor strap or Aunt Ethel's beautifully embroidered tablecloths is just too hard. We do not want to be responsible for destroying the legacy. Leave that to someone else.

You also have an equally complicated emotional storage locker. You can sort through this if you have the desire and the courage. Our early histories have traumas stored in them. These traumas change the present whether we know about it or not. Trauma has a way of showing up and injecting itself in places we least expect. Our brain stores it all. The good news is, all that history is available to us. We must risk climbing through brain cells to unpack those memories. When you do that, the result is relief, insight, and freedom. Early traumas place limits on us. When we decide to explore, we can release stressors and traumas that have been influencing, distorting, and holding us back.

You remember you had a severe accident when you were one and a half. What you do not remember is the surgery and recovery and the four weeks in the hospital with only limited access to your parents. As an adult, you hate hospitals and do not like going to the doctor, but you have never wondered why. You just assumed hospitals are not very welcoming places, plus they smell of disinfectant. Your parents never told you about the brush with death when you were a toddler, so the connection to hating hospitals could not be made. Then you found some old records while going through the family home after your Mom's death. Wow! Unpacking paid off.

REFLECTING

1. Describe your earliest memory.
2. Write about a recent trauma or problem.
3. Ask your parents to give you a clear history of early childhood. What other trauma experiences do you find?

2. BISCUITS AND GRAVY

A recent pop quiz that jumped into my Inbox showed a picture of a stack of biscuits, and at once, I remembered my grandmother making biscuits and gravy for breakfast. What a throwback! Her kitchen was huge, the most enormous room in the house. Of course, her family was huge, too. All those hands were needed for working the farm, and birth control was not even a 'word'. The stove was fed by wood, and water was hauled in from the well pump in the middle of the backyard. Biscuits and gravy…daily fuel for the work to come.

When you think of your extended family, what food memories come to mind? Food is fuel, and it is also ritual. We carry some of those rituals forward through the food we prepare for holidays.

Memories of early childhood are enormously important for us. You may not realize it, but your brain holds on to your life experiences from birth and even before birth. Our brains are a huge database. That database fuels our day-to-day experiences. As a college student, I remember working in the computer lab with these cabinet-shaped units that filled a room and these stiff paper cards with little square holes that you had to use to feed the machine data to analyze. If our brains had to be constructed in the same way, the planet would not have space for very many of us. Imagine if your history had to be stored on these cards. We can all be grateful for the unique quality and capacity of our brains. Imagine if we had to read these cards for your history to release the emotional impact of life experiences, and free yourself from habits, hurts, and traumas.

This releasing is an important task and enables us to understand our thoughts and feelings as they have been shaped by our history. Our brains store everything. As Science advances, we can demonstrate this quite easily. When certain sections of the brain are stimulated electronically, images, sounds, stories appear spontaneously. When you realize that your brain stores everything, you must stand in awe. You also get to take advantage of this fact to understand parts of your history and to heal from injuries.

Few of us really want to go back in time to examine an injury. However, going back in time to examine an injury has tremendous value. When we carry these earlier traumas and injuries without examining them, they will change the present in surprising ways.

Many of the generational traumas we carry are painful. These traumas can be woven into belief systems, carried in traditions and rituals, and exercised in actual behaviors. Think of the Colonial beliefs that females were not to be educated. How much brainpower was wasted on that one! Then we have the tradition of the first-born male being treated as the next head of the family regardless of his talents or intellect – which led to some disasters.

We all have these early experiences where some resources are missing, or some family tradition is conducted blindly. We make an adjustment which becomes a process we repeat to our detriment. As we progress in life, we continue to use this method even when it is unnecessary, does not apply, or truly undermines us. I like talking about the biscuits and gravy that made up every one of Grandma's breakfasts, but I would never eat that combination again! Way too salty!

REFLECTING

1. What early memories have been brought up for you?
2. Examine how that early memory changes you in the present.
3. Examine how that early memory impacts those around you.

3. STAY OPEN TO THE FLOW

When I first heard this phrase, I was unsure of the meaning or intent. Was I about to get flooded with streams of water or overrun without resistance? What should I expect? I need an explanation here before I can proceed. Am I blocking opportunity or damming things up? So, I decided to take the phrase apart.

STAY

Stay is a familiar command to any dog owner. This is one of the first commands that you teach as it relates to safety. Someone was encouraging me to be safe or to at least watch for danger. I am doing something that needs to be stopped because it is too risky. The command could also relate to remaining in a comfortable place. How often have you been in a place where you just want to stay? I know that feeling of peace and safety. While you know that you cannot stay, to think about staying or remaining to be surrounded by safety is compelling.

OPEN

Open is an invitation. A genie is creating magic and opening a new space or adventure for me. Might I meet Aladdin in a gold-filled cave? The invitation is like a familiar neon sign, letting me know that I am welcome and invited in. The local tavern could be beckoning me to sit and enjoy the atmosphere. It could also be an instruction for me to be open, and to examine the places that I need to expand and be accessible or show interest and acceptance. I know that history can create closures that need to be examined and revised.

FLOW

My first thought about the concept of flow is to imagine the running of a river as it passes in front of the cottage. The flow of the river is constant and mesmerizing. The sound is gentle and hypnotic. I imagine where I could go if I put a canoe in and paddled along the river. Might it take me to gentle curves or torrid rapids or throw me over a waterfall. Then I reflect on the flow of lava that I recently saw on the television and pray for the survival of hundreds caught in its fiery path. Some flows can bring destruction. How would I respond to that? Do I have the ability to rebuild?

UNDERSTAND YOURSELF

1. Are you choosing the life you want to live?
2. In what ways are you open to adventure or change?
3. Where are you really going?

4. SNOW

As the snow falls, the sight is quite mesmerizing. Do you ever wonder where those flakes come from, or how far they have fallen? Snow develops when the atmosphere is cold enough to form ice crystals around dust particles in the air. We get entertained by the sense of floating and dancing in the air as it falls. Once on the ground, the snow protects small plants against the cold! I had no idea. Once accumulated, snow entertains children and some adults and frightens others, causing genuine inconvenience.

Why is snowfall mesmerizing? The shape of those flakes is fascinating, and snow comes in different forms as well. Today's snow is light and fluffy, while other snowfalls are wet and heavy. People can be like that as well. Who do you find fascinating in your life? Who lights up the room upon entry? Who is heavy and weighs you down?

We often do not allow ourselves to let the heavy ones melt away, particularly if they are family members. As the snow falls, it sticks to the trees and bushes and piles up on the outdoor furniture. This morning, I was fascinated by the snow piled on the slats of the outdoor rocker. The snow accumulated in perfect prisms on each slat. Fascinating!

I was reminded of science experiments in elementary school with prisms and bending light into assorted colors. Light, like people, can be complicated. We may present as simple, but the truth is we are all full of complications and different shades that blend in fascinating ways. As the snow accumulates, I wonder how my presence is accumulating. When with my family, do I present as an attractive "shape" with a history that can mesmerize or entertain? Can I change the shape to create different atmospheres and appeal to others? When do I present as heavier, wetter, and soggier? Who are the heavy ones in my life? As I reflect on the heavy ones, I am not fascinated. I am burdened and must decide what to do next.

Of course, I realize I am not a snowflake, but I am fascinated with the possibility. How do I change shape for different situations? I know that I do. The professional me is focused and engaged in my work. My attention is fully on. The hobbyist is playful and experimental. I am willing to try new things to see what will happen. The teacher in me is organized and able to challenge the students not only to have fun with the lesson but also to take home just one nugget that will stay with them and hopefully have an influence. The family of origin part of me is distressed by sibling rivalries and troubled times. How will I relate to these troubles?

When I watch the snowfall, I am reminded of the infinite possibilities that await us all. Like the snow, we are shaped by the "dust," the unsavory parts of our lives, and at the same time, we reflect the light in fascinating and mesmerizing ways. We accumulate experiences; sometimes, they stick with us for a long time, and other times, they melt quickly away. We can get stuck and overwhelmed and must dig ourselves out. We can also glide over our troubles and ski right through the dangers. And like the snow, we have a history and a future.

REFLECTING

1. Who are the heavy relationships in your life?
2. What parts of these relationships do you need to change or let go of?
3. What needs to take their place?

5. HAPPY HOLIDAYS!

Hannukkah, Christmas, St. Nicholas Day, Feast of the Immaculate Conception, Bodhi Day, Feast Day of Our Lady of Guadalupe, Yule, Boxing Day, Kwanzaa, Zarthost No-Diso, New Year's Eve. One would be hard-pressed to find another month with as many holidays. Whatever your belief system, the intent is remembrance and connection. Each holiday is a time to come together, cease the everyday routine, or lay aside conflicts to focus on a higher form of existence. At least once a year, we carve out time to focus outside ourselves and remember we are connected somehow to a purpose beyond our present.

Fortunately, I have a model of that in my extended family. My Aunt Myrtle was that type of woman. She never saw the labels people carry and often cherish. She never saw the skin tones that divide so many. She knew how to open her heart to others. Her expression of acceptance was often fulfilled at the dinner table. I remember when I was in middle school, our family was going to her house for dinner, and I had a friend visiting. I did not want to send my friend home, so we called Aunt Myrtle to see if an extra plate could be added to the table. My Aunt graciously said yes and asked, "What is her favorite dish?" My friend reported macaroni and cheese as her favorite. When we arrived for dinner, a big bowl of macaroni and cheese had been added to the already full table.

That is indeed a higher form of existence. I know many people would say, "Sure, bring her along," and they would set an extra plate and drag a kitchen chair into the dining room. I am still looking for someone to ask about my favorite dish and then go to the trouble to make it. Lest you think this came out of a box or the frozen Stouffer's meal you get in the freezer department at the grocery, it did not. Aunt Myrtle would never have done that. Boiled macaroni and handmade cheese sauce was whipped up for my friend. Of course, we all enjoyed it!

When you have family at your house, I hope you will think of this story and ask yourself what you could do to honor each person who is expected. No matter the holiday you are celebrating, remember the purpose is the connection with others. Celebrations bring us together and allow us to honor one another. How will you open your heart to do that?

Read, Reflect, Respond

REFLECTING

1. Holidays can be complex. Take time to write about their impact on you.
2. Given this impact, what needs to change?
3. What action will you take to bring about change?

SECTION 3

CONNECTING WITH OTHERS

1. BEING INCLUDED

When our friends make plans, we want to be included. When we arrive home from school or work, we want to be expected and greeted with interest. That greeting can change the tenor of the entire evening. We need that attention. Yes, I know there are times that we want to be alone. We want to reflect or puzzle on our own. However, we were born connected to another person, and we seek that connection throughout the rest of our lives. We are social beings to our core.

Much of our early social training takes place in the kitchen. This is where we get trained to meet challenges and become competent. The early task of setting the silverware and napkins is simple but has a much more powerful meaning. In that simple task, I am being trusted to place things properly; I am operating independently; I am serving others; I am being acknowledged for my contribution to the greater whole.

When we have completed the task, we will be noticed and thanked for our contribution. That simple appreciation accumulates into a sense of self-worth. We like being noticed. We want others to be interested in what we have done, how we feel about it, and what we can accomplish on our own. As we mature, our responsibilities increase and become more complex. The kitchen is the training ground for responsibility.

The kitchen can also be fun as we learn to make cookies and cupcakes and follow recipes. A friend of mine makes bread every week, and her grandson delights in measuring the flour and watching the yeast expand before it is added to the mixer. And who can resist the smell of freshly baked bread?

One of the first places that a child experiences inclusion that gives the child meaning and importance is in the kitchen. The kitchen gives opportunity to experience responsibility. Family traditions are often born in the kitchen. The bread you make on the weekend or the cookies that fill the tin may be a child's introduction to being included in an important family ritual.

Special occasions are celebrated around the table. The special cake for a birthday may be your tradition. Thanksgiving is all about loading the table for everyone to enjoy. We never really lose our desire to gather in the kitchen and share time together – no matter how old we are. From the beginning, our desire to be known, valued, and appreciated is baked into us.

REFLECTING

1. How did your parents include you in family responsibilities?
2. What are your memories of growing up in the kitchen?
3. How have these early experiences shaped who you are today?

2. "INDIAN SUMMER"

Here on the East Coast, we are experiencing an "Indian Summer." Winter is delayed by summer and Spring-like temperatures – we have been on the porch enjoying the warmth and breezes. Of course, there are days when a sweater is required or a blanket across the legs is handy, but we are outside. A few last blooms from the garden still provide a sweet scent, and the serenity bell vibrates with a slight breeze, sharing tones of deep rest.

We know Winter is coming, yet we stretch to stay outside longer, hoping the Fall foliage will hang on for dear life. The leaves on the birch tree have turned a soft yellow with a tinge of orange, and the peeling bark provides a gorgeous canvas as a background. I want to stay outside just a bit longer. I want to hang on for dear life.

I am not a winter person. I do not ski or snowshoe, and we never get enough snow to build that snowman from my childhood in the Midwest. I do enjoy a fire in the fireplace, though, despite the task of hauling wood from the woodpile and tracking pieces of bark across the floor. Yet, I would much rather be outside. What are you hanging onto for dear life? I bet it is not weather-related.

We hold onto objects. My mother collected antique pitchers. When she passed, I listed many of them on eBay. I kept a few which were her favorites or had sentimental value because they were gifts or inherited from her many sisters. My father collected tools and gadgets. He passed them to my husband, who culled through them. He still has the large wooden toolbox my father used as a tool and die maker in his craft.

Objects, whether jewelry, paintings, photographs, records, or furniture, capture our attention. They can be small or large, valuable or straight out of the claw machine. I gave each woman a teddy bear for fun at a recent luncheon with friends. One of them took two home to share with her recent twin granddaughters. We were thrilled when the girls played with them for over an hour. The joy of finding pleasure in an object is a treat not to be missed.

Our home is filled with these treasures, and no matter how many times we think of culling through them to save our children from that task when we are gone, we fail to release any of them. Being surrounded by objects that bring memories, comfort, or joy is a treat.

When I see one of my mother's pitchers or a porcelain box my husband gave me as a gift, I am flooded with valuable memories. So, Sorry, daughter. You will have to call in the antique dealer or the junk guys because I am not culling the family history collection.

REFLECTING

1. How do objects connect you with others?
2. How conscious are you of why you hold onto these objects?
3. Where is the boundary for you between collecting and hoarding?

3. ICED TEA

I remember summers on the porch; invariably, the pitcher of iced tea would come out. In the heat of the summer, nothing tasted better – the tea was Lipton, of course. It had been steeped for precisely three minutes then poured into the big pitcher filled with ice. There were no tea bags. Those came along later. You had to be careful to confine the tea leaves to this mesh ball with a hinge on it. When you poured the hot tea into the pitcher, it made a crackling sound that was quite satisfying. While some ice melted with the hot liquid, plenty remained to cool the beverage for a long time.

The porch was the place to gather. Every house on the block had a front porch with a swing. Of course, our home also had a big back porch with another swing, but that is a story for another day. As the day cooled down and the neighbors came out, people wandered down the sidewalk onto the porch for a chat and a taste of your iced tea. The visit would last from a few minutes to close to an hour before the neighbor moved on – depending on the neighbor and the topic of conversation. These evenings were better than the party line.

Do you remember the party line or even know what it is? When I was a child, the telephone was affordable because you shared a telephone line with a few neighbors. Each neighbor had their ring on the party line, so you would only pick up if the number of rings were for your house. Now, I know what you are thinking, and yes, it did happen. If you wanted to listen to your neighbor's call, you would carefully pick up the receiver. If you picked it up quickly, it would make a noise, and the neighbor could tell you to get off the line. If you were successful, the results could be pretty juicy!

Sometimes the neighbor would "hog" the line, and some pretty heated conversations were had. But most of the time, the phone was a great convenience. Now, we carry a phone around in our pockets. Everyone has one, and the age of getting one keeps getting younger and younger. They make these simple flip phones for toddlers where you can put a picture of Mom, Dad, Grandma, or someone else, and all the child must do is press the image to start a call. That is early training on using a phone.

Most young people never use their phones to call. They use them to text their friends or surf the platforms where you can watch little snippets of someone doing something silly or stupid. I have often seen two teenagers sitting beside each other, each typing away on their phones. When I asked one what they were doing, I discovered they were texting each other! Yikes. I prefer the iced tea on the front porch.

REFLECTING

1. What are your memories of neighbors from your childhood?
2. Who are your neighbors now? Can you name those within a block radius?
3. What kind of neighbor are you?

4. YOU CAN MAKE FRIENDS WITH A FLY

A lovely friend tells me this was her mother's description of her as a child. When I heard it, I laughed. I could not help myself. Then, as life often does, a fly came into my life. When we pulled out of the driveway to travel from Chevy Chase, MD, to Tysons, VA, about a 35-minute drive, a fly was on the windshield in the driver's direct view. As we traveled, we marveled at the continuing presence of the fly and began to talk to it. That fly was still there when we pulled into the parking garage. And yes, he was alive and proceeded to fly away. What was he doing? Staying in place for that length of time at highway speeds seemed impossible. Perhaps he was there to remind me of my friend's story. Did we make friends? Did he like me? He certainly held on for a long time!

I know you have had this experience where you meet someone for the first time, chat briefly, and feel connected. As the conversation ends, you think, "That was lovely. I want to get to know that person." Something inside of us gives us a nudge to gravitate toward one person or another. When I work with couples, I see the nudge is often to be attracted to someone with the characteristics or qualities experienced in one parent or another. We are driven to replay the family drama and improve it. For some couples, this is productive and healing. For others, it is a disaster leading to pain and separation, or a life of constant stress and misery. Spouses do not always end up being friends.

The sense that a new person would make a good friend is in a completely different category. Friends can be deeply attached, but at the same time, there is a boundary or a distance as we inevitably go our separate ways and live separate lives. This reality may be the very reason maintaining friendships is so much easier than maintaining spouses. The time away allows us to reflect on the positives as well as to forget the negatives.

Some parts of us resonate or vibrate with the sense that this potential friend would be interesting to know, great fun, or important in our lives. Our brains are figuring this out on our behalf. Our brains are marvelous organs. They are constantly problem-solving and seeking connection and resolution. Even when we are sleeping, our brains are problem-solving. They are redecorating the room all the time. They move bits and pieces around to see how they fit together until they find the better sequence or the more significant idea. Often, I have awoken with a new idea or with the solution to a problem which seemed unsolvable the day before. I am so glad my brain works on my behalf. Even though I could make friends with a fly, I would much prefer making friends with my brain.

REFLECTING

1. Remember your first friend? Tell the story.
2. What role do friends play in your life now?
3. Who do you need to befriend?

5. FOOD FROM CHILDHOOD

What was your favorite food as a child?

Of course, you may have to think in categories: favorite lunch to take to school, favorite Thanksgiving dish, favorite dessert, favorite snack. They are all important. My daughter's favorite lunch from preschool through high school was a peanut butter and jelly sandwich—every day for years! One must wonder if it was tasty, easy, or always traded for other things. Finally, the sandwich is currency! My favorite food growing up was infrequently made.

My mother made these excellent crescent rolls for special meals. They were not the kind you get from that funny can you must whack on the side of the counter to get the dough to burst open. My mother's recipe came from her mother, who undoubtedly got it from her mother. They were light as a feather and buttery, so these fluffy things would melt in your mouth. And you could not stop with just one. I am fortunate she only made them for special occasions. If they had been weekly baking, I would weigh a lot more!

My mother also made Banana Nut Bread, which I loved. It smelled so good, and everyone was drawn to the kitchen as it was baked. Once, I got in trouble for secretly eating a "can" of this stuff. When my older sister was in college, my mother would send care packages, which invariably contained a baked sweet. Mother had a clever way of sending the banana nut bread so that it would arrive safely. She baked the bread in gold-lined tin cans. I have no idea why some tin cans were lined with this gold-colored coating, but Mother thought that made them safe to bake in. I benefited from this belief. Sneaking into the kitchen, I would carefully remove the baked bread from the tin can, cut off the bottom portion, stuff the can with waxed paper, and replace the top. Voila! Of course, the college recipient on the other end was not pleased. And yes, I did get in trouble.

Think about your favorite foods from the kitchen. Memories from childhood have a purpose, and they can pop out of our brains at exciting times. Food is famous for triggering memories from childhood. I realize some of you may have harrowing memories that come to the surface. Those are valuable, too. They take more work and sometimes need to be shared with a therapist or close friend to receive proper care. Painful memories are essential parts of our history, just like pleasant ones. Our brains store these things for a reason. When we bring them out into the open, we have an opportunity for care and healing. Some of these painful memories contain lessons we can now understand. They can help us set boundaries, make changes, and grow in our understanding of ourselves. Memories are supposed to be "visited." Some visits bring us pleasure, and some show us pain which needs to be addressed. Open yourself up to both.

REFLECTING

1. What foods were important to you?
2. How were those foods important to you?
3. What do they help you understand about yourself, your relationships or how you want to live your life?

6. BOARD GAMES

When you were a child, do you remember playing board games? When you had your children, did you play board games? As an adult, do you play board games? A good board game is tons of fun and can be played by a few or many. You may not know that board games have a deep history dating back to ancient times. Who knew they had so much leisure? One of the earliest board games was found in Egypt, dating to 3,000 BC. Yes, you read that right…. BC!

Pictures of the game and players have been found inside ancient tombs. The game has a thirty-square playing board and a collection of pawns. The board looks like a cribbage board with a drawer for storing the pieces. Aside from a few ancient drawings, there are no directions on how to play the game. However, I still say it looks like cribbage, which my husband consistently wins. So, it is not a game that I want to learn!

Board games are designed for fun and competition. I can still play a mean Scrabble game with my granddaughter. She is an avid reader, so sometimes we must drag out the dictionary. I frequently get stuck with the Q, which is deadly. Board games are designed for all ages. You played Chutes and Ladders with your toddler or were a Candyland fan. The point is games bring us together in ways other things do not.

Some games can be played with all ages. Others, like chess, require time to learn and become proficient in. Whatever game you choose, the goal is to gather and have fun. You can play as individuals, partners, or with the right combination of people; any board game can become a team sport.

Board games can go anywhere with you; some have even found their way to your phone. The fascinating thing about board games is that they continue to be invented. Some of the new ones for 2024 are interesting. While I am not endorsing any of these, I am intrigued by the names and sequence of play:

Mycelia is a strategic mushroom game. What could be better than hunting mushrooms? Does anyone die from a poisonous one? Third Crusade is a team-based game with battles and crusades fit for Kings. Scarce is a cooperative action-based game with a weird spinning board. You may not go for a brand-new game, and I do not blame you. I like to stick with the oldies, and Monopoly can go on for days!

REFLECTING

1. What is the earliest game you remember playing, and who played with you?
2. What role do games play in helping you connect with others?
3. What other activities do you use to connect to others?

SECTION 4

WORKING WITH OTHERS

1. BAKED INTO THE CAKE

I love to bake. It is just one of my favorite things. I also love my KitchenAid Stand mixer, mainly because it is pink. Equipment is critical to a good bake. When focusing on the kitchen, we take our equipment quite seriously. There is a favorite wooden spoon or a few for different purposes. Then comes the pots and pans with specialty bottoms; just the right one for browning steaks and the special griddle for pancakes. In the kitchen we are thoughtful about our equipment. The garlic press must be efficient and effective because my knife skills are not to be trusted with chopping garlic. I want to preserve my fingers, and that clumsy press is too hard to clean, so the roly-poly press is just the thing.

What equipment do we use when working with others? If you visit a professional kitchen, you might be surprised at the scale of the equipment. My KitchenAid would be swallowed up by the huge mixer that sits on the floor as though it were a round bathtub. I have often envied the range in the kitchen at the Inn at Little Washington in Washington, Virginia. I believe the range is French and the handles must be polished daily. You can reserve a table in the Kitchen to get a firsthand look at how all the marvelous dishes are prepared. Kitchens evoke memories of warmth and joy as you anticipate the treats that will be prepared.

The kitchen requires cooperation and coordination. My brother-in-law and his wife started their cooking together in the tiniest kitchen that I have ever seen. I swear it had to be a broom closet before a stove and sink were inserted. And the fridge was a tiny under-counter thing that would require you to make trips to the grocery every day. Yet they managed an elegant dance in that tiny space and produced luscious meals. Obviously, the kitchen has no bounds. Big or small, the guests can be well served.

Some professional kitchens find the head chef throwing language and tone around as though they were in a war zone and about to be attacked. The pressure of creating delicious elegance can lead to tension as the kitchen must produce meals swiftly.

The opportunity to train and to love is so present in the kitchen. When a child is old enough to reach the table, it is the perfect time to give them the responsibility of setting the silverware and napkins. As they grow, they get to set the plates and glasses. The power of being included, expected, trained, and appreciated cannot be underestimated.

REFLECTING

1. Write about your earliest memory of being in the kitchen when you were included, trained, and valued.
2. Review the times and ways outside the kitchen you have been wanted and included, trained, and appreciated. Describe the impact on you?

Gloria Vanderhorst, PhD

2. SAILING

How do you feel about water? Yes, I imagine you drink it. The recommended daily consumption is 15.5 cups for men and 11.5 cups for women. I have a water pitcher by my side all day. However, I am obviously behind the times as I drink eight glasses of water daily. I am sure that if I hit the 11.5 for women, I would float away, never to be seen again.

I would much rather relate to water quite differently. I prefer floating in the pool or doing laps. I love every minute in the lap pool. When it gets busy, you must share a lane, but if you swim in different directions, there is only a moment when you must be careful not to collide.

One year, I decided to experience the water from a different vantage point. Luckily, I lived in a lovely harbor town, and the sailing school had plenty of space for new learners. Classes were about half a day every Saturday, and I loved it. We would do the book learning and testing first and then get into our boats. Beginners start in small, single boats with one sail. The harbor was calm and safe, so tooling around in your little boat was easy.

I will admit that occasionally, two students would collide, but these little shells were hardy, so no damage was done. In this small boat, you learned to feel the wind, adjust your sail to capture the most wind possible, and then tighten or loosen the ropes to make turns. These were great learning devices.

Moving from the single to the larger boats with a crew of four meant we had to cooperate with others and take turns leading the crew. While this might sound like a piece of cake, it was not. Groups, even small ones, can take a lot of work to manage. The four sailors need to work in rhythm with each other. You cannot clone yourself to build the crew, so you must work with three different people. Even though each person takes a turn as captain, you would be surprised at how much "backseat" sailing takes place in a 4-man crew.

As the class proceeds, you begin to figure out who to put in the boat so you can have a successful sail. Cooperation and coordination are essential. If you are not coordinated, you can capsize a sailboat. I have been in the water that way once, and I do not want to go there again. A four-person crew can right a boat, but it takes work. That was the best cooperation we ever had.

Like anything in life, sailing takes knowledge and cooperation. Bringing a crew together is not easy, but the result is glorious! Sailing out of the harbor just before sunset is one of the most beautiful and serene experiences. You may not be a sailor, but finding that spot where your skill brings you joy is well worth the capsizing.

REFLECTING

1. When working with others, how do you cooperate?
2. When you capsize or fail at something, what do you do?
3. When you must regroup, who do you depend on to support you and why?

3. GUILT

Let us face it: sometimes we feel guilty, which is a good thing.

Have you ever wondered why your brain has this ability to experience something you are doing and at once start wagging its finger and telling you it is an unbelievably lousy idea? Who programmed the brain to know? How does it know? Can I shut this part off?

We come into this world with an innate ability to know when we have crossed the line and are doing something wrong. Great programming. Still, why do we have this program automatically loaded into our brains? It is excellent preparation for being in a social environment. Without it, we might regularly commit mayhem. Still, at times, it can be just what we want to do – even if we do feel bad. This means aggression is also a fully loaded program.

We must figure out how to live with both.

This form of aggression, the ability to shame another, is always available. As teens, we tend to use this with regularity. When we become teens, our brains like to experiment with various "fully loaded" programs. Boys make fun of each other in the locker room. Girls tease each other about romantic interests. We get our licks in. As adolescence wanes and we emerge from a hormonal fog, we look back with regret.

I remember a friend who was a talented musician talking about the torture he delivered to some peers in high school. He was one of the "cool guys" who played guitar well and attracted the girls. He enjoyed picking on the lesser guys who were nerdy or had no talent to set them apart and could not attract a girl. As an adult, he felt genuine grief about those teen interactions. I admired the next move he made. He found the guys he tortured and apologized. That took courage.

When we are the guilty party, courage is always required. This is a skill that must be practiced. Apologies are not easy, and many of us do not do them well. Somehow, we tend to explain or justify rather than take responsibility. It goes like this: "I know I was a jerk to you, but I didn't know any better." Really! Are you trying to say you were not born with a conscience? "Sorry, we came into the world with one of those too." Check yourself on this the next time you apologize.

The guitar player was able to take responsibility for hurting his peers. That apology also relieved his guilt and led to healing for him and the guys he had shamed and tortured. I admire his courage and willingness to make amends. When we truly embrace ourselves and take responsibility for who we have been and what we have done, we grow into ourselves and become the people we were designed to be. To whom do you owe an apology? Make it soon.

REFLECTING

1. Who have you shamed or teased?
2. If you have taken responsibility, how did you do it?
3. If you have not taken responsibility, how would you do it?
4. Now, express a time when you were the target.

4. ARE YOU A CONNECTOR?

We all long to be connected and accepted by others. That longing is planted in us even before birth. Yet sometimes our families do not seem to know what to do with that longing. Given the universal nature of this desire, knowing how to do it should be second nature. However, this desire which is so natural is sometimes not met with the knowledge of how to do it. Some families are oblivious to teaching their children how to make meaningful connections with others. This training starts at birth.

We cry for a variety of reasons and often our parents can read those cries with ease. When a parent struggles to interpret the infant's cries, the system of communication breaks down and frustration sets in for both the child and the parent.

We are all physical beings, so think about this. We have been in a womb where all parts of us have been touched constantly as we float in a fluid environment. No wonder we like to return to fluid environments: the swimming pool, the ocean, the bath, the shower. If we could, we might always float around or enjoy being wet. Remember "Singing in The Rain" and how young children like to jump in puddles? We describe it as "floating on air" when we fall in love. We tend to like being touched especially when that touch mimics that sense of floating or being supported. Toddlers spend a lot of time climbing on their parents and siblings, too, if they are available. Increasing our awareness of the importance of touch is enormously important. Our skin is the largest organ in our body! Think of the significance of that. As we are touched, we are nurtured, and those good chemicals get released in our brains leading us to feel a sense of closeness and value. The simple act of touching another can send healing chemicals throughout our brains.

That is not surprising when you put it into the context of being created in a supportive pool and loving the experience of continuing to float around, be it in the tub, the pool, or the ocean. When are you "floating"? Take that experience seriously and expand on it. Find ways to experience the world as your support system, as though you were floating. Starting at the world level may be too ambitious. Let us talk about growing into the support systems that are readily available to you. First, we would look to our family of origin for meaningful connections. Even in the most difficult of families, we can often find a kindred soul. Sometimes siblings play this role. Sometimes, a grandparent, cousin, or uncle stands at the ready if we are only willing to take the risk.

Growing into the support systems that are offered to you can be a challenge. If we have been hurt by others, we tend to withdraw and imagine that every relationship carries the same risk of pain. The challenge is to look around, anticipate, expect. Our own thoughts often draw the attention of the other resulting in a connection. Be present with those who love you and support those that you love. You were born connected. Grow into those **connections.**

REFLECTING

1. Describe your support system and how it works.
2. Reflect on "touch", both how you offer it and how you receive it.
3. Where do you need to grow?

5. AWARENESS

We are all familiar with this word. However, have you ever really stopped to figure out what it truly means? The police caution us to be aware of our surroundings. Our friends wonder if we are aware of something that is happening in the social group. Our spiritual guides want us to be mindful of other dimensions beyond ourselves. The neighborhood naturalist wants us to know about the flora and fauna and how we care for other creatures. The full-length mirror in my bedroom wants me to be aware of how I look. My colleagues want me to be mindful of my impact on others. My mother, if she were still here, would want me to be aware of my language and what I am eating.

Awareness is a state of being. Mahatma Gandhi has a quote that illustrates awareness for me. "Live as if you were to die tomorrow. Learn as if you were to live forever." If you were to die tomorrow, what would today look like? Your first thought might be that you would eat as much ice cream as you could. However, your next thought will go to the connections that you have made with others. You will want to be with those you love and spend time connecting, remembering, and advising. You will want to laugh and cry. Would you pick up a book to learn one last thing? How much time do you devote to learning in your current living state? Are you curious about a variety of areas of life and knowledge? Do you challenge yourself to investigate new concepts such as Artificial Intelligence? Let awareness inspire your curiosity and drive your quest for knowledge, including understanding the implications of AI on human interactions.

Artificial Intelligence, or AI, is everywhere. When I draft an email, the AI highlights better phrasing or catches misspelled words. This thing is fast, too. I must admit that I have relaxed into it and appreciate the errors it quickly catches. However, I am not sure I know what will happen next or where this intelligence is leading. Robots in fast food places that man the fryer can save humans from grease burns and provide a financial break for the store owner, leading to more profits. And, yes, I have seen the clips where robots learn to play soccer. However, I cannot imagine going to the stadium or the ice rink to watch a bunch of robots engage in a sport. But that is where this innovation will lead. In the future, AI is expected to revolutionize various industries, from healthcare to transportation, and even create new job opportunities in fields we cannot yet imagine.

How can I be more aware of what is happening around me? To whom am I paying attention? Who am I neglecting? Am I likely to be replaced with another or with a robot? Will that awareness help me to prepare or just scare me? I can imagine robots replacing people in many ways. Assembly lines are already teeming with robots. Now, a robot can serve my fries, and I can expect to check out through a machine as well. What will be the impact of not having that 2- or 3-minute exchange with the cashier? What will be the impact of reducing those small human interactions? As we face the increasing presence of AI, let us not forget the value of these small human interactions that add richness to our lives.

REFLECTING

1. Familiarize yourself with Ghandi's philosophy and describe what it means to you.
2. Familiarize yourself with AI and describe what it means to you.
3. To whom are you paying attention? Who are your neglecting?

SECTION 5

MAINTAINING CONNECTIONS

1. BUILDING A RESERVE WITH OTHERS

How often do you get frustrated with someone? How does frustration show in your relationship? Working in a group can sometimes be particularly problematic and frustrating.

When each person is vested in their own ideas and plans, the tension increases. You have been there more than once. I know I have, and sometimes, it makes me wonder if the group process is worth the aggravation.

Organizations can be unwieldy and complicated, as though they are mazes you must get through, and there are so many dead ends that you get tired of retracing your steps and trying a new path. I think about the giant corn mazes in the country. They look great from the air with their lovely patterns and shapes. Yet, when confronted with those stalks and paths, disorientation comes quickly. Suddenly, we are all alone and lost. We are born connected and seek connection with others as a natural state of being. Thus, we hope to find our way out of the maze and to be welcomed and connected.

People always recommend patience. Yes, I get it, but what does that look like? What does it mean? I am lost in this maze and want out! My patience is escaping. How often do I experience a model of patience I can adopt? One of my dear friends has found the solution to frustrating interactions. She makes a commitment to others and herself that I genuinely admire. Here is her sage advice:

"None of us is perfect, so we have patience with others to build up a reserve with others, hoping that reserve will be used towards us when we need it."

Oh, what a beautiful sentiment and such wisdom. Perhaps seeing patience as nuggets of gold will help me accept the frustrations. I do not have to lean into frustration or worry. I can imagine those deposits building up and envision my little Fort Knox.

We all need reserves. When I think of consciously building a reserve, my own Fort Knox of tolerance and acceptance, I find it easier to face the frustrations. Someone has intentionally left me out of the email string. Ouch! She wanted to gather support before presenting the idea. OK. That still hurts. We like to be included – inclusion gives us value. When I think of this as a nugget for my Fort Knox, where I can offer patience to the one who was afraid of my reaction, I can do a better job of letting go of the frustration. I hope others are building their own Fort Knox in their relationships with me. I want others to be patient with me. I know I can be overbearing at times and neglectful at others.

I want to be offered grace and the opportunity to maintain a connection. If I am truly honest with myself, I want them to give me a second and a third chance. Thank you, friend, for that sage advice.

REFLECTING

1. Who frustrates you the most? Express how this impacts you.
2. If you were to choose to be patient with this person, what would change in your behavior? And in their responses?
3. When has another person built up a reserve with you? How was that manifested?

2. ARE YOU YOUR OWN CON ARTIST?

Whoa! Why would I ever imagine you are a con artist? Those people go around fooling others and taking advantage of them. Bernie Madoff was a con artist, and I am not in his category. He took conning others to an art level. Is not his name hilarious? He "made off" with so many people's money for so long! But I am not talking about that kind of deceit but about self-deception.

We tend to have ways of conning ourselves, which could be more subtle, attractive, and successful. We long for the stable, the predictable, the comfortable. Yet, let us take a step back and look at our lives as they unfold. We must notice the inconvenient, frustrating, irritating, disappointing, and, yes, deceptive. We tend to call the deceptive "little white lies." How often have you told someone you are unavailable for lunch or are not feeling well and will catch them next time? Oh, now you know what I am talking about! We all need to be more transparent.

Often, being transparent is thought of as being "brutally" honest. Why the focus on "brutality"? Is honesty really that dangerous? Can I be honest and still maintain a connection with another? Why do we think honesty will disrupt a relationship, bringing relief and increased closeness? Why do we want to protect ourselves so much? What would happen if we were transparent? Imagine the following exchange and track the feelings that come up for you.

"Susan, we have hung out together for a long time, and throughout that time I have changed and grown, and you have stayed the same. When we chat, you tend to review the same stories I have heard. You have serious problems at work and in your marriage that hold you back in several areas of your life, yet you are unwilling to seek help or create change. I love you, and at the same time, I feel helpless in enjoying our time together. I must make a change and am not interested in our weekly chats as they are happening now. I want to change the friendship and not lose it. I want to discuss how you can be proactive and grow emotionally so that our friendship has more depth, and I want to see whether we can find a more satisfying way of being together".

Wow, would that blow you away? Or would it be an open space for you and your friend to use to be more productive, social, or intimate with each other? Trapped-transparent is hard, but feeling trapped by a dynamic is even more challenging. Being transparent comes with risks.

And it also comes with rewards.

My friend Susan has a choice; she can accept some modification to our friendship – it does not have to end. It just must change. Or she could walk away from the friendship, which may not be my intent or my need. I cannot spend two hours a week listening to the same stories and providing the same empathy. Change is risky, but if you stay in that rut, you are conning yourself and your friends. So, I will ask again: Are you your con artist?

REFLECTING

1. Reflect on your relationships and write about one that frustrates you. Be honest.
2. If you used your courage to confront this frustration, what would you say?
3. If you stay in your current dynamic with that person, how will you show patience and tolerance?

3. FRIENDS

I love having friends! They send you marvelous things you would never find on your own. I like the email messages with some small articles attached, the funny pictures, and the serious ones of their child's wedding. My friends expand my world. We are born connected to another person, and we spend the rest of our lives working on making connections with others. Remember your first friend in school or your neighborhood?

I know people who have friends from the toddler group their mothers first took them to. I admire the ability to keep in touch with someone who met you when you were in diapers. It is a remarkable history to go from playing with blocks and soft, squishy toys through the angst of teen years, the separation from high school or college to adulthood, and still be connected. Who is your longest friend?

Maintaining friendships takes time and energy. The payoff is that you are "known." How often do we want to be known or seen? From the small parts of life where we want our friend to remember that we miss our grandchildren, to the big scenes where we want our boss to mention our work and effort on our latest project, and how well it turned out. We all want to be "known."

How does this "knowing" happen? Have you ever wondered if you are sharing too much? Can you see others shrinking when you go into deeply personal places they are not ready to receive? Or do you hold back and not tell your stories for fear others will distance themselves from you, not be interested, or go as far as to behave as though you have not shared at all?

I know you have had one or all these experiences. We want to be "known," yet the process is not always straightforward. When this becomes difficult, do you persist or withdraw? How can we tell which is which? Reading the other can truly be difficult. Building a relationship takes time, and we must accept that we will stumble and recover and stumble and recover until a bond is formed and each of us can be trusted.

The key to building this relationship is taking risks and being transparent while respecting your friend's wants and needs. Recognizing the boundaries of the other is an essential part of creating a friendship. When you cross your friends' boundaries, you need to be able to receive feedback respectfully. We have boundaries which enable us to feel safe, confident, and whole.

Your friendships are a vital part of your life, whether they started when you were a toddler or just this week when new neighbors arrived. We all need to be connected. Some of us seem to do this with ease, while others must be truly conscious of how and why to do this. Where you fall, developing a friend or a network of friends is critical for physical and mental health.

REFLECTING

1. Reflect on how you function as a friend.
2. Select one of these relationships as your focus. Write about the longevity, importance, depth, and meaning of this relationship in your life.
3. What would you like to change about this relationship?

4. AARDVARK

This may be an odd title, but the story bears telling. When our daughter was three or four, we attended a large indoor crafts fair at the Montgomery Fair Grounds. The space was huge and filled with booths of wonderful handmade things. As a small child, she was mesmerized and found numerous things which attracted her eye: paintings, glass, furniture, and so on. To help her focus and stop requesting everything she saw, her father told her he would buy her an aardvark if she could find one. This was a safe deal as none of these craftsmen were likely to have an aardvark.

She was now laser focused. As we "oohed and aahed" over many different things, she politely requested an aardvark at each booth. We came to a booth with various stuffed animals, but thankfully, no aardvarks were on display. When we thought we would skate free, our daughter politely asked the vendor if she had an aardvark. With a look of surprise and shock, the woman asked why she wanted an aardvark. Our daughter proceeded to explain the contract. "Ahh", said the vendor. Then, she bent down, and from under the front table, she pulled a sizeable 5-foot-long aardvark! There it was! A stuffed aardvark. I love my husband, but I genuinely admire him here. True to his word, he bought an exceptionally large and extremely expensive aardvark!

How we treat our children is critical. Keeping a promise and fulfilling a contract is an act of pure respect. There was no waffling or backpedaling. The deal was done, and the aardvark had a new home. What are your aardvarks? When have you made promises and tried to back away, compromise, or just flat-out refuse? We often think that we can renege on our promises to children. They are small and young. They will get over it. They are not likely to remember. WRONG! Maybe this is why we are disappointed and irritated when they do not listen or follow our directions.

Honoring our promises shows them being trustworthy and connected is essential. In my work, parents come into the office when they have exhausted all their other options. The parents complain their teens will not listen to them, quickly break the rules, and escalate to doing risky things. I see the pain and fear, and I know this dynamic did not start in adolescence. This present dynamic has a history to it. So, I began to look for the "missing aardvark." Invariably one exists, often several. The parents have not given any weight to these earlier dynamics. The child was just young, so why would a promise or agreement need to be honored? What if it was inconvenient? Or it was just too expensive, just like the aardvark.

How we treat our children accumulates. The defiant teen is not an anomaly. Mom and Dad have been working on this for a long time. Repairing the damage is difficult. It would have been so much easier to buy the aardvark.

REFLECTING

1. When you make promises to your family, especially to your children, how often do you keep them? Give an example of keeping a promise and an example of changing your mind.
2. When you make a promise to someone not related to you, how often do you keep it?
3. What experiences of broken promises or assurances do you need to address?
4. How will you go about doing this?

5. HALLOWEEN

Do you remember being excited about Halloween? Of course, the big draw is collecting candy and often having contests with your siblings or friends to see how much you have collected compared to them. The build-up to Halloween is exciting as you think through who or what you want to be. There are so many choices. Will you be a princess or a Pokémon character or go as the "Jack of Spades" or some animal you admire? Regardless of your costume, the fun is running from house to house to see what the goodies will be.

Occasionally, the neighbor surprises you with a scarecrow that jumps out of the bushes or makes a scary sound as you push the doorbell. The experience is both thrilling and shocking. At the end of the day, stories of these adventures will be told and replayed in school tomorrow.

Halloween has been celebrated for centuries. It began as a pagan ritual by the Celts to commemorate the harvest. In the eighth century, Pope Gregory modified the pagan tradition to honor all Saints, thus giving it the name All Saints Day. The evening before All Saints Day was designated as All Hallows Eve, which has been modified into Halloween. Therefore, a mixture of pagan and religious beliefs forms the Halloween we enjoy today.

One of the favorite things for many families is to carve pumpkins. These can be big or small. The roadside stalls display a variety of pumpkins, and selecting just the right one for your vision is an art. The carving can be messy, and there is debate about keeping and roasting the seeds or tossing them in the garbage. This endeavor is genuinely messy as the inside of a pumpkin is a stringy, gooey mess. Watch out for the mischievous child who decides to sling some of this stuff at their sibling! This is an outdoor activity if the weather is warm – or should be contained in the garage. Many parents have been left cleaning up the kitchen after a carving extravaganza.

Pumpkin contests also exist. Gardeners spend months overseeing the growth of these gourds to take home the honor of growing the world's most giant pumpkin. In 2023, this honor went to Travis Gienger from Anoka, Minnesota. His pumpkin weighed 2,749 pounds! And somehow, he transported this thing from Minnesota to Half Moon Bay, California, for the official weigh-in! The word is his pumpkin could produce 687 pies! Wow!

And yes, making pumpkin pie is also a Halloween tradition.

REFLECTING

1. Choosing a "character" is an expression of your sense of self. Review your costumes for insights into yourself.
2. This holiday is a group experience. How do you function in groups?

SECTION 6

OBSTACLES TO CONNECTING

1. BODY OF WORK

Do you realize each of you has a "Body of Work"? We tend to think only famous people have Bodies of Work: Books, poems, artwork, music, inventions, discoveries. All progress in the world around us has been dependent on these "bodies of work," and we are grateful for the wheel, the jet engine, the atomic clock, and the rocket that has taken us to the moon and back.

However, the truth is we are building a "Body of Work" every day. Now is the time to take responsibility for yourself. You have a body of work in your profession, even if it is staying home and caring for your family. You have a body of work in your community. Even if it is keeping your lawn mowed or helping the elderly neighbor next door get to a doctor's appointment. How will your neighbors talk about you, share their understanding of who you are, or remember you when you move?

Your "Body of Work" is your BOW in the current world of acronyms. Now, depending on the pronunciation, we can go in one of two directions. Let us start with the one which describes the front of a boat. The bow is upfront and takes the lead, which also means it takes the brunt of the forces the boat is encountering. What forces are you meeting? How are you "taking" them? The bow is designed to cut through these forces carrying the boat forward in search of better places. When you meet waves of challenge, pushback, and confrontation, I hope your bow can face them with dignity, security, and fortitude.

Now let us look at a different definition: BOW...to yield or bend. What happens to you when you are placed in the position of bending to the other? Do you do it with ease and grace when you yield on the highway? When you must yield in a relationship or pause to wait, the deference to the other does not seem easy. Discerning when to bow and when to fight can be exceedingly tricky.

Yet, we all experience a time when we must bend. We are capable of it. At the same time, the emotion that floods us is often a powerful resistance, as though we will be broken entirely if we bend. We should be more aware of our resilience and recognize that in discerning when to bend, we are gaining an opportunity to examine ourselves more closely. Personal growth comes from knowing when to yield. When you must give way, I hope you can do it gracefully and continue to move forward.

Moving forward and cutting through the waters that would overpower or misdirect us must be done. When facing a challenge, we must navigate our lives in ways that move us forward and learn to give way to others when their path is better. Our "body of work" depends on how we BOW.

REFLECTING

1. What is your "body of work"?
2. Where do you have to push through to continue your "body of work"?
3. Where do you have to bend? How good are you at doing this part?

2. YOU CAN MEET SOMEONE ONLY AS DEEPLY AS THEY CAN MEET THEMSELVES

I love it when clients teach me new things or say something in a way which strikes me so profoundly, I want to share it. This is one of those phrases: "We are born connected to another human and spend our lives seeking connection with others."

We often search for that best friend with whom we can relax and be soooo comfortable that we lose track of time and ourselves. We settle into a rhythm which reminds us of the steady heartbeat from the womb: dependable, subtle, and comfortable. We long for a space where it feels right, and we know we belong. We long to know each other and to be known.

We want a best friend, the one person who will be there for us no matter what. Who will get our jokes and laugh with us, listen to our complaints, and validate us, hear our longings, and encourage us. Someone who knows our weaknesses yet keeps us honest. Who sees us flagging and pushes us forward. Meeting that friend requires meeting yourself.

You must investigate your early experiences, see the child in you, and know your history and needs. There are times when that child rushes to the forefront and takes over now because some early experience has injured you or frightened you. When this happens, do you realize your childhood is about to take over your present? Can you meet this part of yourself and understand what has sent the child part rushing into the present? Will you acknowledge the need or the pain? Or will you let the past take over and drag you back into childhood behaviors and feelings? To know yourself is to know all the parts of your history and how those parts seek expression in the present. To know yourself is to question and evaluate whether you need to react from that younger self.

Each of us has many parts. Occasionally, one of those parts can take over the whole. I want to increase my awareness to meet those parts and consider what they need now, and how I want to relate to those earlier parts. I want to meet myself and work through those earlier dynamics. I want to keep the pieces that help me in the present and release those which cause harm to me and others. I can only do this once I am willing to scrutinize the past.

Meeting your early history is not easy, and many times, you will need a guide, a therapist, or a trusted wise elder. Facing your history and how it can jump into the present takes work. Doing this in any meaningful way requires support. We are born connected to another, and to transform from being in utero to being in the world, we need help. To convert from being stuck in past behaviors, thoughts, and beliefs, we also need help.

REFLECTING

1. Reflect on your childhood memories and pick one to describe.
2. How does that experience function today in relationships and in terms of having that best friend?
3. Look at that experience from another angle. Examine the impact it is having on those around you who might want to be closer friends or a best friend.

3. HUMMINGBIRDS

Every summer, we put out a hummingbird feeder, positioned so that we can see it from the kitchen table. Interestingly, it always takes them a few weeks to find the thing. Once they do, they come at the same time each morning and late afternoon. As the summer ends, they frequent the feeder more often. I understand they are "bulking up" for their migration. They will soon be headed to the Caribbean, and I envy them. The same birds tend to return to the same places year after year. We are considering building them a house! We will put a "welcome home" sign on it as well.

One came right up to the sliding glass door this morning and hovered there, staring at me as if to say, "Why are you sitting still? Why don't you get ready?" Then, I had to wonder what I was ready for. I no longer go to school, so I cannot get ready for that like all the kids in the neighborhood. I am not migrating anywhere. I am likely to be planted here forever. Like the giant Sycamore tree in the yard, I have deep roots and will not likely move soon. So, as we stare at each other, I wonder, "Where does this bird expect me to go?!"

Where do I expect myself to go? I am old, so my "go machine" may be rusty. Then I remembered that I go for connection. I want to be with others. I want to laugh, tell stories, and share the books I have been reading, the places I have been, and the daydreams that circle in my head.

I regularly have lunch with a group of women called "my lunch bunch." We gather to laugh, plan adventures, and discuss the latest personal, local, and global news. We are a force to reckon with. I may not be headed to the Caribbean, but I am indeed headed toward friends and fellowship. Like the hummingbird, I have my "charm". Yes, that is what a group of hummingbirds is called. They are not a flock, a crowd, or a mob. They are a "charm". Well, that is just charming, and from now on, my friend group will be a "charm."

I know I have said this before, but it bears repeating. We are born connected to another person and spend our lives seeking connection. We are social beings and need connections to strengthen ourselves and prepare for the journey ahead. Our connections with others energize us, comfort us, and sustain us. We want to be connected and enjoy the company of others. We need time to ourselves, but isolation is not in the cards. When isolated, we tend to go off the rails. We are social beings, and that is just plain "charming."

While my curious hummingbird can be protective of the feeder and wants his own time on the perch, it is also a social being and just wanted to see if his inquiry would stir me to action.

REFLECTING

1. How do you connect with others?
2. Where do you go for connection?
3. Why do you connect with one person and not another?

4. FALSE EXPECTATIONS APPEARING REAL

We all experience it. Let us examine it from the perspective of the phrase above. Are our worries false expectations that are real? Sometimes that is a perfect fit. We imagine if we go to the neighborhood barbecue this person will not like us or will tend to ignore us. We are reluctant to walk down the block into an experience of rejection. Or we submit a resume for a job we want but believe there will be so much competition ours will land in the round file.

Our expectations shape so much of our lives. The teenage boy who expects to be rejected will not approach the pretty girl he admires across the room. He misses the opportunity to connect and begin a relationship. He imagines she is too cute to be interested in him. He thinks he is not "cool" enough or he will have no idea what to say to her despite sharing two critical classes with her, giving him lots of ways to start a conversation. Years later, he shares this moment with her at the class reunion, and she remarks that she liked him too! Yet, they never took the risk.

The college senior who is so anxious about job interviews, he skips the on-campus fairs where employers come to interview graduating seniors. He misses the opportunity to practice interviewing, or to find a good fit for his future. Fear trumps the value of experiencing multiple interviews and allowing practice to reduce that fear. Who cares if the first few are awkward? Practice will always be informative and shape how we do the next time.

In my practice, I have often heard a woman lament the things she did not try. She may have liked science but decided the coursework would be too challenging, so she stuck with general studies and majored in something which was not challenging at all – however, she was likely to land a job upon graduation. In her leisure time, she reads non-fiction with a scientific interest. She has missed her place in the world and does not like her job.

What happens inside of us when we stop risking? Think of how many times a toddler lands on their butt in the quest to master walking. What if we let the first crash stop us or define us? We would all be crawling or sliding around on our butts!

REFLECTING

1. Name the thing you fear the most. Write/draw it over and over.
2. That fear has caused me to miss the following.
3. When I let go of that fear, I will be able to…
4. I will do the following to address this fear and end it.

5. ANCIENT ROME HAD FEMALE GLADIATORS

Yep. You read that right. Women were gladiators! Huge crowds came to see the gladiators. This was a well-attended sport, much like football today in that people came to see strong, muscular individuals face off against each other, crash into each other, and stop their opponent from advancing. The opponents fought a bloody battle like today on the gridiron and then resigned from the field. No one died. They lived to fight another day and please the crowd again as they cheered and shouted, hoping the opponent would be crushed and humiliated. And just like the Romans, we call this sport. Why do we enjoy watching people face off against each other and work to destroy each other? The culture must benefit from these shows of strength and threats of death. Of course, most sports on the television today do not end in death or even carry the threat of death. However, the rabid experiences of fans as they support their teams can get mixed with alcohol easily and though the gridiron or stadium may not be violent, some watch parties are.

How does this viewing help us? We all want the strength to defeat our enemy and advance victorious. The female gladiators show us that women can entertain with violence just as easily as men. Shows of violence must serve a purpose, as they have been popular for centuries. The spectator may have the experience of releasing thoughts and feelings of aggression by watching shows of violence, thus leading to a more negligible probability that the spectator will commit acts of violence. However, I wonder where the cost/benefit analysis breaks down or crosses a threshold.

Why do we enjoy watching people face off against each other and work to destroy each other? What do we gain by watching people face off, shove each other around, and dominate the other? This is an essential part of human culture, or it would not have been going on for centuries and show little or no sign of abating.

The culture must benefit from these shows of strength and threats of death. We all want the strength to defeat our enemy and maintain our presence. Sports are not the only entertainment venues based on threat and violence. Murder mysteries can be intellectual, like Agatha Christie or Sherlock Holmes, or violent contests like The Hunger Games, which has a series of films with murderous challenges. Challenge, advancement, and triumph, even on a small scale stimulate something in our DNA.

The spectator may have the experience of releasing thoughts and feelings of aggression by watching shows of violence, thus leading to a more negligible probability that the spectator will commit acts of violence. However, I wonder where the cost/benefit analysis breaks down or crosses a threshold. Since we are now introducing violent games to younger children, we should pause and wonder if it has a different function for younger children.

REFLECTING

1. Each of us has a need to compete in some way.
2. How does your competitive part show up?
3. Competition can sometimes spill over into violence in thought or action.
4. Think about your relationship to violence and describe it.

SECTION 7

CONNECTING WITH FAMILY

1. GROUNDHOG DAY

OK! You know about Groundhog Day, right? If you grew up in the United States, you have celebrated this for years. But do you know why? This tradition has been going on for 138 years as of February 2024. Did you know it is celebrated in Canada? We long for Spring and need a predictor of when it will arrive. Right?

The chosen groundhog lives in Gobbler's Knob, Pennsylvania, and is called Punxsutawney Phil. Every Year this town goes wild for the event that will predict Spring. The whole town gathers at sunrise to see the groundhog emerge from its winter sleep and observe whether it sees its shadow or not. If he sees his shadow, we are in for six more weeks of Winter. Brrrr.

Of course, this is not a 138-year-old groundhog. He is a relative of the original. German immigrants brought this tradition with them, and even though they depended on the badger in Germany, the immigrants found the groundhog to be an excellent substitute.

Remember your first day of school when the teacher becomes a substitute for your parent? Of course, the teacher plays a different role in your life, but the teacher does substitute for your parent in many ways. The teacher gives directions and expects compliance. The teacher comes to your aid and, at the same time, expects you to try. The teacher develops routines and expects you to follow them. Somewhat like the groundhog, the teacher is ever-present Year after Year and into adulthood. The label may change to supervisor, mentor, or boss, but the dynamic remains the same.

Traditions are an essential part of our identity and a way to pass on our heritage from one generation to the next. Traditions give us a sense of grounding and belonging.

We all need to feel connected, and regardless of how serious or silly the tradition is, it serves an essential purpose in the fabric of our lives. Traditions form a bond with others as we participate and honor the tradition. The bonding we experience helps us to feel important and valuable, even if the tradition is silly. The townspeople in Gobbler's Knob, Pennsylvania, have been genuinely persistent in their tradition. And people all over the United States and Canada who tune in on the morning of February 2 each year are honoring a tradition. Groundhog Day is important. What would we do if they stopped waking this creature to see how he predicts the weather?

REFLECTING

1. What traditions do you value in your family? Which ones seem silly or embarrassing to you? Take time to research the history of these traditions.

2. GRANDCHILDREN

What is it about grandchildren that is so special? Have you ever wondered about this? People seem to light up when they talk about their grandchildren. A change in their faces makes their complexions glow a bit. Of course, they are proud of their children and can tell you the latest news about their sons and daughters. But when you ask about their grandchildren, they glow.

I have a friend who is a model grandmother. Her four children live all over the country. Each decided to leave their home base and settle in various parts of the United States. As her children had their children, she decided that if she had a relationship with her grandchildren, she would have to go to them. Thus began her grandmother's trips. Every three months, she would go to visit her grandchildren.

Now, you can imagine that as each family grew, her time on the road or in an airplane grew along with her family. Yet, she kept her commitment to herself and built a relationship with each of her grandchildren. She is proud of that accomplishment and blessed to receive love from the far corners of the United States. How do you relate to your grandchildren?

This next generation will see things we can only imagine, just as our grandparents watched us accomplish things they could only imagine. My grandparents lived on a farm and only had indoor plumbing once I reached middle school. The Apollo landing in 1969 was mind-blowing for my grandparents' generation. Several people in their generation wondered if it ever happened. They imagined all the events took place on a movie set. But, sorry, the moon is real. We have been there and come back and plan to go again.

Watching some videos about current incubators where future inventions are being built is fascinating. I saw one invention where the person turned thoughts into words on the page. All he had to do was think, and the computer wrote it out. That is wild. At some point, we may not need to carry our cell phones around. We can think: "I would like to talk to my granddaughter."

Then, wherever she is, this idea will appear on her computer screen. Remember "The Jetsons"? This animated family hit the screens in 1962 with these personal flying machines that took them to work and every place else. We may not be too far from these personal flying machines.

Soon, Amazon promises to drop your packages off from a drone and practically eliminate its fleet of trucks. Who knows what will come next? Our grandchildren will be an essential part of this future. If they are not inventing, they certainly will be the end user.

REFLECTING

1. What relationships are important to you?
2. How intentional are you in maintaining these relationships?
3. How are you encouraging those you love?

3. THE LESSON OF THE MONARCH

Several years ago, in my more adventuresome days, I decided to go to the Eastern Shore of Maryland for a unique festival. In a small town on the coast, they celebrate the migration of the Monarch Butterfly. Each year, the Monarch descends on this town like the locusts of the plains. The difference is that the Monarch comes to feed but not destroy. The bushes are covered with these brightly colored mothlike creatures. Everywhere you look, they are present. They fly together in great swoops making a dancing show as they move through the town. Their orange and black pattern reminds me of Halloween! However, I do not think they are masquerading. They are the real deal.

They spend their days beefing up for the long trip to come. Even though they weigh less than one gram, they must beef up for the 3,000-mile trip from New Jersey to Mexico. They fly to the southernmost part of Mexico, and that qualifies as a miracle. However, these are strange creatures indeed as those heading south to Mexico have never been there before. They are a new generation, and they will make that trip but never return. Next year a new generation will make the return trip north and they will die leaving yet another new generation to find their way south. What a marvelous mystery. The genetic message must truly be strong. One can only imagine how powerful these genes must be.

Somehow the memory passes from one generation to the next. We often find a similar message traveling in human families. Generation after generation can be found in different trades and endeavors. My father came from a long line of farmers. I am sure that you know families that have carried professional traditions on for generations as well.

Families tend to take great pride in passing trades and businesses from one generation to another. Do you come from such a family? We know that physical traits pass from one generation to another. I have a friend who comes from a long line of redheads and is quite proud of that gene!

In general, we tend to take pride in traits that we have inherited as long as we are not talking about inherited disorders associated with some single genes. "By and large", families show pride in talents that have been passed from one generation to another. Families take pride in a variety of arts that move through generations and in superior intellects as well as physiques.

Encouraging a young child to follow in the footsteps of a parent or relative brings a sense of connection to the past and to the future. We are born connected, and we spend our lives seeking connection. When we look at family traits, we can find satisfaction in making those connections. So, if you have talents that you can attribute to an early generation let yourself smile and reflect on how one small gene can carry such a large load. The next time you see a Monarch butterfly, think of how miraculous genes can be.

REFLECTING

1. Reflect on your family traits and inheritance.
2. In what do you take pride?
3. If you could choose, what family trait would you acquire?

4. COLLEGE BOUND

"For those of you who are waiting to receive decision letters and have endured the rigors of applying, January is when most college decisions are made. You have been working towards this deadline for months. Each email or snail mail triggers some degree of anxiety as you await the news. Have you been accepted or not?"

The high school guidance counselor has said these words repeatedly. What factors into these decisions to apply? Families that can afford it have hired a college consultant to walk their adolescents through reviewing colleges, drafting essays, ranking their admission chances, and completing the applications. These teens have been through multiple rounds of test-taking. The tension is high in these households even if everything looks smooth. So many factors go into this decision and the next phase of this teen's life.

Some of you have coached your teens directly on how to draft an essay and where to focus so they are a great candidate. Some of your teens have done this on their own and hope their grades, essays, and descriptions of their future goals will catch the reader's attention and allow them to pass to the next level.

I have had many opportunities to see this play out in families, and I remember my stress as a parent during this time. Launching a child into the "outer" world of college is as complex as launching a rocket into space. Years of preparation have gone into this moment. Some parents think about this day when they send their child to kindergarten. Some only think about it once the high school counselor sends home some forms.

Many have been setting money aside in some form: a state savings plan designated for higher education, an investment account they nurture in the evenings as they watch the market fluctuate, a drawer where they squirrel away cash. Some have not faced the reality of this expense and find themselves either panicking or grieving. This next phase of life is stressful all around. There is a good reason we call it "college bound." Someone in this child's life is bound to pay the price.

The government has recently covered millions of college loans with a debt forgiveness plan. The taxpayer is bound to feel the consequence of that in some way. The student must show up for class and give their best effort. However, the temptation of freedom, Greek life, new relationships, unfamiliar places, and the opportunity to make decisions without immediate oversight is genuinely challenging. This first year catches many of these teens off guard. Some wash out early, struggle to make it past their first year, and some develop new insights and take them seriously. Some come prepared for this transition and are grateful to their parents and high schools for the hard lessons leading up to this adventure.

Whether your child goes to college or not, this time is a rite of passage. Every teen, whether they choose this path or another will be challenged intellectually, emotionally, and socially. As a parent, one hopes that you have prepared your child to face independence and separation with skill and grace. Your high school graduate will be challenged emotionally and socially to discover who they are and who they want to be separate from their family of origin.

REFLECTING

1. As you move through this transition with your teen, look at what lies ahead for you.
2. How prepared are you for the transitions in your future?
3. What preparations should you be making now?

5. THANKSGIVING

So many of us look forward to this holiday for the tasty food and the opportunity to gather with extended family. This holiday has some lovely traditions. The turkey with stuffing will grace the table, and all will "oohs and aahs" at this beautiful bird and its golden-brown skin. Family members will vie for their favorite part and may negotiate or arm wrestle for the drumstick. The cranberry sauce must be authentic and not that gelatinous tube out of a can. The pumpkin pie is necessary, and you can have other pies, but the pumpkin is a given. The table must have sweet potatoes, and a side of green beans would not be frowned upon. Relatives are free to bring other things. You can even bring macaroni and cheese.

This holiday is designed for food. It celebrates the harvest, so all dishes are welcome, even the tomato aspic your Aunt insists on bringing each year, even though half of it tends to return home with her. I suspect she likes this outcome. Providing you do not try the dreaded deep frying of the turkey, your family, and your home will survive intact.

Then there is the football game. One is on the television, and another is in the backyard or out in the street with all the neighbor's kids. What could be better? Do you even know how to throw a football? Do you have an air pump in case the thing has deflated from last year? We are all hoping for nice weather and a spike in the temperature so the crowd can spend some time outdoors before collapsing on the living room floor.

At the same time, Thanksgiving can be stressful because it is meant to please extended family. Do you go to the wife's side of the family or the husband's side? Do you split the day and have dinner in one place and dessert in another? Do you do the Turkey Bowl with the neighbors and then invite both sides of the family to come to your house? Do you alternate years? Of course, these are all things to fight about as well. The family dynamics of this holiday can get sticky.

I wonder if the original Thanksgiving had these same dynamics. The settlers and the Indians were entirely different people with different diets, traditions, and ideas. However, the story is that in November of 1621, the Pilgrims at Plymouth joined the Wampanoag Indians to celebrate a harvest. The Indians brought deer, and the Pilgrims brought a variety of fowl. The event lasted for three days. The local fruit may have been blueberries, grapes, and plums. Mussels were abundant in the area, so they were also on the menu. The whole thing sounds like a real extravaganza. There are no reports of fights or emotional breakdowns. However, most of the women who crossed the ocean did not survive to celebrate this harvest. Seventy-eight percent of the women had died, leaving only four to commemorate this first Thanksgiving. I am profoundly grateful for their sacrifice as I take that fact in.

REFLECTING

1. Do you feel spending the day with family members creates a deeper connection and bond? Why or why not?
2. At family events, people often assume the roles they had in the family as a child. What role did you have in your family growing up and how has that impacted you?

6. BAKING BROWNIES

My mother was an excellent baker. I am not sure if she learned from her mother, though. Her mother was a farmer's wife with twelve children, and it is hard to imagine she had time to bake beyond the basics. I know she made bread and biscuits. The biscuits were a regular part of the breakfast menu, topped off with chipped beef gravy that I will never eat again!

Each Saturday my mother would find something delicious to bake: cakes, pies, cookies, strudels, cupcakes. They were all delicious; you got to participate in the process as a child. Back a chair up to the cabinet and prepare to get your hands dirty. The joy of flour floating in the air and the scent of spices and fruits was fun. You always got to lick the spoon or the beater… Of course, after they were finished being used.

Then came the cleanup and waiting time. When you have participated in making something, waiting is hard. Cleaning up the counter came first, and then there would be time to play cards at the kitchen table until the timer went off. That was a glorious sound! A few long minutes of waiting would be rewarded with something delicious.

We did enough work and running around that the sweets never went to our middles. Each child had a job fit to their size and skill set. The youngest would distribute the napkins. Soon, you would graduate to setting the silverware and dishes, and once you could be trusted, you got to do the glasses and pour the milk. The table was a lively place where everyone got to share their day. What you experienced was valued, and as a result, you felt valued. The tradition of family dinners is disappearing.

The families I know now are grabbing food separately to shuttle children to different practices. Or they are grabbing fast food and eating in the car on the way to a game. The sense of being valued as an equal at the table is being lost.

I wonder about the cost of this change. Moving from the placement of napkins to the responsibility of the breakables was a source of pride. Each person grew with the responsibilities they were given, and each person could see clearly how the family system was supported by their contribution. As this opportunity to grow in responsibility and in connection to other members of the group is lost, I wonder what social costs will come with this change.

REFLECTING

1. How did your family value shared responsibility and participation?
2. How do you now spend time with your family?
3. How are you preparing your children to be responsible members of a group?

SECTION 8

FOSTERING PHYSICAL AND MENTAL WELL-BEING

1. DAFFODILS

Did you know that there are thirteen different classes of daffodils? Not me. Of course, I am familiar with the big yellow ones that come up in the early spring. We have a bunch of those that rise from the pachysandra we have planted around the Japanese Cherry tree. These yellow beauties stand tall, and their trumpet shape announces the beginning of spring. If you listen closely, you can hear them heralding the coming season. We have branched out into the two-colored ones with white cups and yellow petals.

I just learned there are other classes of daffodils in a wide range of colors and sizes.

A master gardener would have a collection covering all the species and hybrids. Plant people are fascinating. If I planted just a few of each variety, my flower bed would overflow. It is time to dig up some more grass! Gardens are powerful. There are so many things you can put in a garden. Gardens are peaceful and inviting. In many ways, they are irresistible. You want to walk in them and explore. You want to see what comes next.

A few miles away, we have a delightful public garden. The pathways wind through flowering trees, arbors by the rose gardens, and across small streams where the waterlilies bob around. The path then sweeps into the sun and makes a wide pass around the pond where waterlilies delight with their serene floating and surprising blooms. The grass sweeps forward, drawing you into a narrow path between the bamboo.

The swishing sounds as you pass through the bamboo open to an enclosure filled with flamingos. Imagine 30, 40, or more flamingos wandering around. As you pass the flamingos, you head into a rose arbor with rows and rows of various roses in beautiful pink, yellow, and red colors. The butterfly bushes at the end of the path remind me that I, too, want to plant a butterfly bush. I want the butterflies to find my garden and entertain me with their brightly colored wings and delicate presence.

I want the butterflies to find my garden and entertain me with their brightly colored wings and delicate presence.

The garden is a place to leave stress behind and be renewed.

REFLECTING

1. Where do you go when you need to contemplate?
2. What is your safe space?
3. How often do you let yourself go there?

2. WHEN WAS YOUR LAST PHYSICAL?

What a question! Rarely does anyone ask you this unless it is your new General Practitioner. Yet, it is a fundamental question for you to ask yourself. When we are children, our parents take us for regular checkups. The school requirement for completing the physical paperwork is why. The government wants to reduce liability before putting a large group of kids together in the same room. So, every Fall, a paper comes home through the internet asking for basic physical details from your pediatrician.

Once you leave school, how often do you get a basic physical exam? Probably not on the recommended annual basis. What is it about self-care that is so hard? We let runny noses and coughs go until they clog up our chests. That pain in the back is just that: "a pain in the back." Except when we have trouble bending over to pick up the kids, then we begin to pay attention. The process often goes like this: we have pain and ignore it; the pain changes to cause interference with our daily functioning, we recognize it and put off doing anything about it; the pain stops us in our tracks and the doctor finally gets a look.

We all fail to realize the delay has made the problem worse. If you had done the annual physical, this may have been caught before we even paid attention to it. The intervention could have been less invasive if you had called the doctor at the beginning stages. Now we are stuck. We ignored it. We put it off. Now, it is a real problem requiring surgery and recovery we can ill afford but cannot avoid.

This is the pattern for most adults. We value "pushing through" and avoid "being smart." When it comes to our physical care, we need to be more careful. Our employers should take a page from the school system and require annual physicals. Would that be a considerable money-saver overall? We could be better at self-care.

Of course, our physical well-being is only one part of how we need to care for ourselves. Our mental health is equally or even more critical. Given how good we are at putting off our physical care, you can imagine where attending to our mental health falls. Adults tend to take themselves into therapy only after prolonged periods of distress or when their families demand it. Self-referral as a preventative measure is rare. By the time adults enter the therapy room, much damage has already been done. The "triage" can be complicated. The treatment can be longer than needed, and progress can be hard won.

Your emotional health is directly connected to your physical health and vice versa. We have yet to devise annual emotional exams, but we should consider the value of mental and physical checkups. Being an adult is challenging and demanding. Taking your physical and mental health seriously makes this stage of life so much easier.

REFLECTING

1. When was your last physical?
2. How do you care for your physical body? Be specific.
3. How do you care for your mental health? Be specific.
4. What changes will you make moving forward?
5. What resources do you need to make these changes?

3. AGING

OK! I get it. This is no one's favorite topic. But guess what? It happens to all of us, from the moment we are born, we age. Regardless of how you number the aging process, it happens. We need to be prepared.

The preparation starts way before we begin to think about aging. When you start your first full-time job, one of the pieces of paper you get is information about your company's retirement plan. You can contribute part of your salary. If you are lucky, you will work at a company that matches your contribution or places a fixed amount in your account regardless of whether you contribute. If you do not work for a company that offers a retirement plan, I strongly advise you to begin your own. The amount that you set aside is not important. The important part is that you recognize that your working days will end and that you need a nest egg to tap into.

I know that is looking far ahead, yet this planning is real wisdom. You may not have thought about it and might lament that some of your paycheck is going into a retirement plan, but this is good. You will age. Hopefully, you will live a long life, have a loving family and good friends, and retire when ready.

Most of us do not think about aging. Yet, the truth is we are constantly aging. One might wonder why the body does this, but we are continually at this point. There are efforts in research to develop drugs which can slow this process, but not yet reverse it. Therefore, we must prepare for the fact that our bodies are going to age. Not too many of us take this seriously. Walk through any Mall or Downtown shopping area, and you will see most of us are overweight and out of shape.

The part of us that is constantly aging seems delighted by this phenomenon. Those extra pounds speed up the aging process and place us at risk for various things which will kill us way before our time. Retirement which used to be at 65, is now pushed to seventy. Programs which exist to help us lose weight thrive and are always filled with customers – but not us. This is unmistakable evidence that we do not take our bodies seriously. We rush them forward into early aging.

I love it when the news finds someone celebrating their 100th birthday or even more. Invariably, there are more women than men in this category, and the women are skinny! If we could investigate their photo albums, we would discover they have always been skinny. So, if I want to hit a hundred, I better get skinny. I would not mind hitting a hundred. I can imagine all the new things that will be invented. Our cars will be automatically controlled, and there will never be another accident—unless the computer goes haywire!

REFLECTING

1. Look at your extended family. What factors have influence, longevity or the lack thereof in your extended family?
2. If you could live to be a hundred or beyond and be in good health, what would you most want to experience?
3. How are you caring for your body now?
4. What do you need to change?

4. CALENDAR JOKE

"I can't believe I got fired from the calendar factory.
All I did was take a day off."

OK! A friend of mine from Canada sent me this, and I thought it was so cute. When have you taken a day off and suffered the consequences? We all need days off. I am not just talking about the weekend. Sometimes, the body must take a break and rejuvenate from work and stress. When was the last time you permitted yourself to relax? That could mean taking a brief break from the stress in your life, taking a walk at lunchtime, or just not going to work one day and scheduling a massage. Have you ever scheduled a massage? If you have not, then you are long overdue. Trust me. Your body needs this type of attention.

Do you realize the largest organ in your body is…. your skin? Yep, that is correct. How many of you got it right? Your skin is the largest organ in your body. Having it touched and soothed can go a long way to experiencing physical and emotional health. Touch is a primary need. Do you realize infants will die if they are not touched? They can be well-fed, clean, and healthy, and they will die if they are not touched. The same thing is true as we age. How many elderly relatives do you have? How often have you sat with them? How often do you touch them? How often do you send them a note or a card to tell them you care?

As we age, we get wrinkly, which tends to put people off. They are less likely to put an arm around you, hold your hand, stroke your arm, or hug you. Yet touch is the most powerful sensation. Think about the older people you know and decide to touch them somehow. A hand on the shoulder or resting your hand on theirs can be a gift to that older person. If you want to give them a gift, schedule them for a massage.

You also need to be touched. Take time to give yourself this pleasure. When walking through the neighborhood with your spouse, reach out and hold hands. When talking with a friend, reach over and touch them somehow. Touch their hand. Touch their knee. Touch their shoulder. Take time to be physically present with others. Taking time to care for yourself and connect with others is powerful. Look ahead on your calendar and find a place to take a day off. Be intentional with yourself. Often, I encourage clients and couples to set time aside each quarter to honor themselves. You may spend the day reading that book you have meant to get to. You may go to a museum or a park. You may take yourself out to lunch! "Just take a day off."

[1]*Source:* www.humorthatworks.com/database/funny-work-jokes-to-get-you-through-the-day/

REFLECTING

1. Write about the last time you took a day off.
2. Plan a day off. What will you do?
3. Write about how your day off went. What did you learn?

5. RAKING LEAVES

Do you remember doing this as a kid? With the invention of leaf blowers, the rake has disappeared. Fall used to be a time when everyone was out in their yards raking leaves. The scratch of the rake on the ground was an invitation to all children to come outside and jump in the piles of leaves, then rake them up and jump again. Now the leaf blowers shove the leaves to the curb, and this big truck comes along with a suction tube and sucks them into the trailer. Do the leaves miss those kids jumping into them?

With modernization and innovation, we are missing some essential traditions…and a lot of fun. I remember these two neighbors who lived across the street from each other. Every Fall they would dutifully rake their leaves and put them in bags to be set out on the curb for pickup. However, each would sneak over to the other's yard and invariably dump a bag of leaves on the other's lawn. These guys were hilarious. Every Fall, we would watch this exchange. Sometimes, the dump would occur in the middle of the night or early morning before heading to work. The trick was not to be seen! I miss those guys.

When I was a kid, you could burn your leaves rather than bag them. The smell of burning leaves is lovely. A trail of light smoke and the scent of nature streaming through the neighborhood was delightful. Today, the loud buzz of the leaf blower has taken its place. I understand some municipalities have banned those noisy things and required that they have mufflers. Thank goodness. The sound of a leaf blower is obnoxious.

The other thing we still need is the opportunity to contemplate. The repetitive act of raking is quite conducive to reflection. As you scratch the ground and gather these crunchy things together, the rhythm lulls you into this contemplative state where all sorts of problems can be solved. Remember your fight with the boss or when you forgot an important date? Suddenly, solutions emerge.

Modern inventions have taken away some valuable experiences. The opportunity to do something repetitive is an opportunity to contemplate and reflect. In our more modern world, those spaces are disappearing. Our time is filled with work, commuting, taking children to numerous activities, and rushing to meet the next responsibility, leaving no space for contemplation.

Something important has been lost. We were unaware that certain routines gave time for contemplation and reflection. The solitude afforded by these tasks was valuable. It is time to remember and reconstruct the time to reflect and be with ourselves and nature.

REFLECTING

1. How are modern "conveniences" placing limits on you or making life less rich?
2. When and how do you spend time in reflection?
3. Where does reflection take you?

SECTION 9

UNDERSTANDING CHANGE AND GROWTH

1. DO INFANTS UNDERSTAND EMOTIONS?

From birth, the infant's brain can fully process emotion, enabling them to respond to all the experiences in their environment. Infants cry as they come into the world because they are aware of a change from the womb's protective nest to the world's unfamiliar open-air vastness. They cry to announce they are aware of the change. They sense their protective environment has been dramatically changed and announce their awareness with gusto. They are solely dependent beings and need to draw attention to themselves for survival. Unlike other mammals, they cannot find their mother's milk alone or cling to their parent for attention. Their voice is the mechanism that lets them announce their need to be protected to survive. Building a new form of a protective environment becomes a relational task and the infant is immediately active in creating this.

As evidence of their awareness and active pursuit of care, imagine a well-fed and clothed infant abandoned outside of a church or police station. Instead of remaining calm, the infant is immediately aware of the absence of the adult and will at once begin to cry. They sense a significant other has left them and know they must find other caretakers quickly or they will be in danger. In this way, infants are emotionally brilliant and immediately aware of their surroundings.

Infants hold positive experiences in the same way. You end up with body memories stored in terms of muscle tension or relaxation, internal discomfort or comfort, and visceral reactions. When you experience parents with their infant, you can see the infant's response when tension exists between them. Invariably, the infant will move and fuss and show signs of processing the tension in the environment. They try to shift the parents' attention away from the conflict and toward their needs. This is a valuable survival mechanism.

Infants are emotional sponges because they depend on the external environment for survival. Aware of danger or tension in the environment, they will respond with discomfort and a desire to meet their dependency needs. They announce they need the adults in the room to be focused on them. An angry adult will not be a safe caretaker, and an anxious adult will miss essential signals from the infant.

Infants are excellent barometers of family harmony and tension. The fussy infant often announces something is lacking in the caretaking they are experiencing. When we attend to the infant's signals and take them seriously, we can use these signals to provide an environment that enables the infant to thrive.

REFLECTING

1. Collect pictures of you as an infant and study these pictures to describe what you see.
2. What are the family stories about you as an infant?
3. How do you think your treatment and experiences from birth to two years old have shaped who you are today?

2. APRIL SHOWERS BRING MAY FLOWERS!

Do you remember hearing this when you were a kid? Do you know its origin? A bit of Googling will soon uncover various sources rivaling the flora. One origin comes from 1157, the poet Geoffrey Chaucer penned a version that translates as: "When in April the sweet showers fall, that pierce March's drought to the root and all, and bathed every vein in liquor that has, the power to generate therein and sire the flower."

Things we hear as children need to be challenged. Take the story of the young woman preparing to bake a ham. She cuts the ends off the ham before putting it in the oven, and her friends ask why she does that. She replies that her mother always did it that way. They ask the mother, who replies that her mother did it that way. They ask Grandma, who replies, "I only had one pan, and the ham would not fit unless I cut off the ends."

How are you cutting off the ends of your ham? Take a moment to find your "ham" stories. One of mine caused tension in the first stages of my marriage. We ate dinner together, and as soon as he swallowed the last bite, I cleared the table to start washing the dishes. My husband complained he wanted to sit and talk. I replied we could talk after I finished washing the dishes. Where did this come from?

My mother whisked plates off the table as you finished your last bite, and sometimes even before. I am sure she had reasons buried in the need to complete a farm chore before dark. But I did not live on a farm. However, the angst of letting those dishes sit was painful. My husband had to make the point by letting them sit overnight! In the end, the lesson was worth the pain. Prioritizing the relationship over the dishes was the right thing to do.

What are your "ham" stories? How have they gotten in the way of your friends and family? Take time to examine your "ham" stories. No matter how whacky they are, our parents and other adults embedded them in us at early ages. Before adolescence, we think concretely and see the world in those dichotomies of right and wrong, good, and bad. While this may be a helpful structure for us at incredibly young ages, the world is more complex. Adjusting our belief systems to the more complex and complicated adult world is challenging.

The only path to meeting the challenge is to confront the source. How did you learn it? From whom did you learn it? Does it fit the time? We are all reluctant to challenge these beliefs and systems from our formative years. But wouldn't you like to have the whole ham?

REFLECTING

1. Find your own "ham" story. What have you accepted at face value? Examine its effect on you.
2. Family traditions can cause us harm. What are your "ham" stories: the places where family tradition has caused you problems? What "ham" stories are you passing on to others?

3. ARE YOU A GROWER?

Your first response may be, "Sure I have a vegetable garden and weed it regularly." Or I have this lovely windowsill garden of herbs that make my dinner fare taste delicious. Or you may be thinking of a beautiful flower border you tend with care, however. I am not asking about anything associated with soil and water. I am asking do you challenge yourself to grow emotionally. How would one do that? Or, how would you know when you are challenging yourself to grow emotionally?

We do not have a flashing light which goes off when a growth challenge appears. What do we look for? How will we know when the opportunity arises? Our bodies give us signals, but we are just not used to thinking of those signals as challenges to grow. Here are examples of those signals: our skin flushes and turns varying shades of red or purple; our stomachs do a flip, turn, or churn; our legs weaken or give out underneath us. All of these are forms of the "flashing light" of a challenge we are facing. Think of the last time you experienced one of these. What was the challenge? Most of the time, we will be in a situation involving another person and we sense being seen in a way that feels too vulnerable.

Those physical symptoms are important and need attention. Treat them as a flashing light that is warning you to stop and pay attention. The flush of our skin is a sure sign of embarrassment. Most of us tend to brush that away. I invite you to pay attention and spend time looking at that redness in a new way. Your face is inviting you to examine pieces of history. Look for the "weeds" in your story. Weeds are those places where our growth has been tarnished or stunted and instead of growth we are distorted in some way and experience a sense of shame. This often occurs when someone makes fun of us for some characteristic that we have no control over: the color of our hair, our height, the shape of our head, etc. Those teases show our helplessness as these characteristics were not chosen; they just came as part of the package.

The opportunity for emotional growth is to accept these characteristics that we did not choose. Some people do this by tracing their history. When I can look back to generations past and see how my parts have been passed down, I can identify with others who are like me. Suddenly my flaming red hair is a thing of pride and even though it means I must be incredibly careful on sunny days at the beach, I will no longer feel embarrassed. I can also look out beyond my family to find other examples of redheads who take pride in their looks and may even be famous for that mane!

As we connect to others, we grow in understanding ourselves.

REFLECTING

1. When you hear the phrase "emotional growth," what comes to mind?
2. When have you been challenged to grow emotionally?
3. How did you respond, and what was the outcome?

4. SHAME IS A WHOLE DIFFERENT THING

Each of us can page back to times that we have been embarrassed. In some of those situations, we will find ourselves going silent and shrinking into the background to avoid our feelings crossing over into shame. In other instances, we will be explaining and apologizing. In some situations, we will find ourselves laughing along with everyone else. Laughter is good medicine. Laughter releases stress and relaxes the body. Your brain releases endorphins while your lungs take in oxygen-rich air that stimulates your vital organs, releasing endorphins in your brain leading to feelings of joy. The thought of moving from embarrassment to heightened feelings of health and well-being may be strange but it is the perfect repair for embarrassment. When we are embarrassed, we need repair to reconnect with those around us. Remember that we are born connected and seek connection for the rest of our lives.

When embarrassment crosses over into shame, we must be cautious. While embarrassment allows us to accept responsibility for our behavior, seek forgiveness, and experience being accepted despite making mistakes, shame produces negative chemicals with detrimental impact on our brain and body. We call this experience "toxic shame". We experience a disconnect from others and a disconnect from ourselves. We often want to disappear as though we could melt into the floor and never be seen again. That is toxic shame.

Toxic shame happens when those around us reject us or ostracize us for what we have done. It causes us to believe we are worthless and do not deserve to be connected to others. This is embarrassment gone rogue. Feelings which lead us to believe we are not valuable and do not deserve connection undermine the very essence of our humanity. When we experience shame, we need to repair our relationships. That requires taking responsibility for our behavior. This is a difficult task as our bodies are actually rejecting us at the very moment that we need to reconnect with ourselves so that we can reach for connection with others.

Repair and recovery from shame is not only dependent on our ability to reach for forgiveness, but is interdependent on the other's ability to offer grace. Grace is the offer of repair to ourselves and to others. Through grace we can accept responsibility for what we have done, understand the toxic impact it had on others, and offer repair to those we have injured. Through this complicated process we can return to the relationship. Grace embraces us and assures us we belong and are valued. The offer of grace is an active event that brings us back into the relationship.

Sometimes, this is as subtle as a touch on the shoulder or as bold as a hug. Sometimes, it is a clear and concise explanation of how our behavior has offended. Sometimes, it is a message of correction that trusts us to accept responsibility and to change. Grace gives us assurance and validation that we are wanted and belong. Grace is active, bathing our brains in those valuable endorphins that enable us to restore connection.

REFLECTING

1. Recall a time of shame and put your reactions on the page.
2. Describe a time when others laughed "at" you.
3. When you laugh at "others," what happens to you?

5. COMPUTER HISTORY

I know you have a computer because I cannot imagine the world without one. Have you ever been curious about the history of the development of this marvelous instrument that lets you read everything ever written, travel to every place on the globe and beyond, and calculate your taxes as well? Tax season is upon us, but that is a topic for another time. Today, we are looking at the development of this little to gigantic instrument which affects so much of our lives.

Decades ago, I saw the comedian George Carlin in his early days do a side-splitting skit titled "We Have a Baby." He appeared on stage with a ball and chain attached to his ankle. He placed a diaper on the ball and discussed having this "baby" and all the responsibilities. The ball was hurled into the highchair, fed (sort of), diapered, put to bed to nap, and on and on. It was hilarious.

I feel this same dynamic about my computer today but without the hilarity. It goes everywhere with me in some form or another. The desktop, the laptop, and the cell phone are forever present. This invention is attached to me 24/7. I am sure they will soon have one implanted in me so I do all my work and socialize everywhere "hands-free." Being curious about this "baby," I turned to the internet!

Discovery! A woman played a critical part in the development of this electronic monster! Look her up: Augusta Ada Byron was Lord Byron's only legitimate child. The internet is fabulous! As a mathematician, she saw the potential of this machine to move beyond just using numbers to calculate different things. Seeing beyond is the key.

How often are you challenged to see beyond? You do not have to be a scientist to "see beyond." Fathers and mothers are usually in the position of seeing beyond as they observe their children. Your infant is particularly difficult to soothe, and you begin to pay attention to this like a scientist. You start taking notes to consult the pediatrician with accurate details and examples.

You are using your scientific brain to care about this person struggling with the world. You are the reason your child's autism is diagnosed early, and intervention can begin to make a significant difference in his long-term development. You are the father who notices your middle school boy is uninterested in sports and gravitates more toward creative endeavors. For Halloween, he wants to go to the fabric store and make his costume. You decide to take him and see his interest come to life. He is the fashion designer who will one day dress a star. Who would have guessed?

Seeing beyond is a gift and a challenge. Each of us has the potential to "see beyond." This skill needs to be nurtured and challenged. Too often, we get stuck repeating what we have been taught or what was modeled for us. Challenge yourself to see beyond.

REFLECTING

1. Describe your relationship to your computer in all its various forms.
2. How do you challenge yourself to see potential and look beyond the present?
3. How will you change your relationship with your electronics to make more space for your imagination and reflections?

6. WE ALL KNOW THIS PERSON

I am writing this piece for those who have attended school plays, recitals, and fashion shows from when your children were in preschool to when they graduated. At the beginning of the play or performance, the director announces everyone is to silence their cell phones so as not to disturb the event. Further, they request you stow your phone. The school will record or take pictures which will be available to everyone the next day on the school website. Everyone complies and stows their phone except for that one rogue parent. There is always one rogue parent. What are they thinking?!

During a preschool music performance, I remember one father, cell phone in hand, walking up to the front of the stage mid-performance to snap his darling daughter in the front row. What was he thinking? Where do these people come from? More recently, at a performance, the announcement to silence your phones came with the good news the performance would be recorded and sent to everyone who had purchased a ticket. That sounded great.

Imagine the house lights were dimmed, and the performance is moving along smoothly. The stage is well-lit, the music is grand, and each part is well-played. Then the dreaded "camera parent "appears—standing, clicking, and the flash going off. What is she thinking? I wonder what her child is thinking. Is it, "thanks, Mom, that makes me feel special?" Or is it, "Oh no, it's my mom. I am mortified". Or is it "Good grief, I cannot imagine she is doing this again"? This parent has not only created a dilemma for her child, but she has also given the royal "finger" to the audience, the school, and the participants on the stage.

Help me out here? What is she thinking? Of course, every parent in the crowd wanted to photograph their child doing their one valuable line. However, they respected the school's announcement, put their phones away, and placed them on silence. The request was to focus on the event as it happened and let your heart swell as your child took the stage.

This is what that mother is missing. Her heart is not swelling. Her palms sweat as she sneaks her camera out, attracting the audience's attention with the inevitable flash. Yes, she has captured a picture. Yes, she has embarrassed her child. Yes, she has defied the school's request. And she has robbed herself of that moment of pride when your heart wants to jump out of your chest because you are so proud of your child!

I must wonder about this parent's emotional needs and how she has been parented. What leads up to this defiance? What background overrides the school's best intentions? Some of me wants to reach out to her and say, "I am sorry for whatever that painful history is." Some part of me wants to swat her like a fly.

REFLECTING

1. When you are tempted to break the rules, what stops you?
2. How are you instructing your children or others to respect rules?
3. Look at your relationship to rules and describe how you were trained to relate to rules.
4. What rules do you follow now?

7. GRAY WHALE

Did you see the excitement on the news over the Gray Whale spotted swimming in the Atlantic? This whale was considered extinct in the Atlantic and rare in the Pacific. Imagine! Extinct means gone! Dead! Disappeared! Nada! Then suddenly, there it is, swimming leisurely in the Atlantic waters. Where has this guy been? How did this whale get to the Atlantic? Thanks to global warming and the melting of the polar ice cap, scientists believe it could have come through the Northwest Passage, which previously would only have been accessible to a submarine.

The first submarine to travel this path had to go deep under the ice with the fear that a way back to the surface may not have been found. Imagine that experience! Or have you already had that experience? Our lives can sometimes take us into deep, dark places where we question whether we will surface again. Losses can put us under the sea. A friend of mine recently gave a speech about the loss of a child. Just hearing the story came close to putting me under the sea, and she lived it. The natural path of life is to be born, cared for, released to be on our own, grow up, grow old, and then leave. That is the natural order of things.

When the natural order is disturbed, we are thrown off course. Some manage to find a new passage, and some are lost forever. A new passage may take many different forms. We hear on the news about parents who have lost a child and started a charity to help other families with similar problems. We see scholarships dedicated to others lost or memorials established as reminders of those we love. Remembering those we have loved is powerful and essential. That person may be a family member, a friend you depended on, or a colleague you truly admired. Memories are powerful. They can comfort, spur us to action, and surround us with love.

Who are the ones you have lost? How do you honor them? In what way are they swimming back into the present and stirring you to act? You may not have traversed the North Pole, but the loss you have experienced has shaken you to the core. Honoring that loss is essential.

In helping one family through a loss, I asked them to collect things that reminded them of their attachment and place them together in a prominent place in the house. They chose a small table in the front hall. One by one, they brought things to put on the table: Pictures, rocks collected on a hike, a wooden spoon, and old birthday cards. As the collection grew, their conversations grew as well. The stories of engagement, prowess, and silliness replaced the pain of loss. A healing process was unfolding.

REFLECTING

1. What has disappeared from your life and what meaning did it have for you?
2. How have you honored those who have impacted your life?
3. What new paths have opened for you because of any of these losses?

8. CHANGES TO THE LANDSCAPE

Do you remember the big tree in your front yard? The one you would run away to when you ran away from home. The one you would sit under in the heat of the summer and wrap yourself in its shade. The one which dropped all those leaves in the fall, making a pile you and your friends could jump in. The one which would shelter you in the late evening when you played hide and seek.

I remember when its core was rotten and had to be cut down or risk falling on the house. That was quite a day. This massive truck with a giant crane arm parked out front, and this skinny guy hauling himself up the tree with a rope mechanism and a chainsaw dangling from his waist. He hoisted himself to the top of the tree like a monkey and began to lob off branches. When only the bare trunk was left and the chain saw cut was made, the crane lifted the trunk onto the truck bed like a matchstick.

What are the towering trees of your life you have been holding onto despite the signs of aging and deterioration? The familiar can be so comfortable. Take a moment to examine the "big trees" in your landscape of life. Do you believe your tendency to procrastinate is just how it is? Were you just born to put things off? Delay calling back? Are you late for meetings? Be the last one in the pew?

Your "big trees" have roots. They started somewhere, and as you repeated them and repeated them, they became more prominent and stronger and took over space in your life before you realized. Now, you think they are permanent and just the way you are. I remember my sister-in-law who was consistently an hour late for every event. We called it the "Phyllis factor." After a while, we began to give her different information, calculating the lateness into the formula. Sunday dinner would be at 11 a.m. so she would be there when it was ready at noon.

Why did we accommodate her? Why couldn't she see her lateness as an insult to everyone else?

Seeing our rotting trees takes work, and who wants to call in the crane? You are connected to other people, and how you function impacts all those others. The hard part is to reflect and see yourself. When you are standing in front of the mirror, what do you really see? Where is your focus? The next time you gaze into the mirror, take a long moment to reflect on the past week. Ask yourself the following questions: Who has had to wait on me this week? That "wait" could mean time or service. Take a close look at both. Who has been disappointed in me? This could apply to yourself or others. Be honest and transparent. Who have I hurt, offended, or neglected? We all do this, and facing ourselves is essential.

REFLECTING

1. How has your childhood shaped the characteristics that hold you back or undermine you?
2. How are these characteristics causing strain and discomfort for others?
3. What resources do you need to address these and create change?

9. TOOTHBRUSHING

The other morning, I was brushing my teeth and remembered my sister's story of doing the same in California. She reported you never leave the water running while brushing your teeth. You barely wet your brush and barely rinse it when you finish. Take a sip of water to rinse your mouth. The water table in California is being depleted. Between city development, population growth, and farming, the water table is being sucked dry. The water table in California has been dropping for the past two decades. Water conservation is a priority in the State, yet more is needed to divert a disaster. As a result, they are going beyond their borders to draw water from other states. The outcome of such a situation could be disastrous for more than California.

We all have water tables of a sort…. our emotional and intellectual resources. How are you using your "water tables"? How are you using your resources when you face simple tasks like toothbrushing, dishwashing, or laundry? While doing mundane tasks our brains tend to fill the time with processing ideas, problems, or dreams that are way beyond the mundane. Check yourself the next time you do a common task.

When doing mundane chores, our brains frequently process problems and puzzles unrelated to the chore. Pay attention to what your brain is doing. Sometimes I marvel at the protective skull. Have you ever wondered why your brain has such protection? This is a unique organ! No other part of the body has such protection.

While doing mundane tasks like emptying the dishwasher, your brain is busy solving complex problems or creating modern designs for that house project you are planning. You might say the brain has a mind of its own. I have often heard someone say a solution to a complex problem came to them while showering. The brain likes the rush of water or the sound of rain. Our brains are always busy. Even when we are sleeping, we are processing the events and stressors of the day. Sometimes, I encourage clients to keep a notebook at their bedside so they can write down snippets of dreams. Our dreams are how our brains organize, react to, and sort out the events of the day – and the trials in our lives. They can be quite helpful in showing us the feeling we may have dismissed in our busy day. When you wake up and go to brush your teeth, think about what your brain may be telling you about the strains of the day and your resources for addressing them.

REFLECTING

1. How are you relating to your natural environment?
2. Now think about your internal environment. What do you find? What emotions, memories, or injuries are hanging around?

10. ANESTHESIA AND SLEEP!

If you have had surgery recently, you know the effects of flushing this stuff out of your body for a few days afterward. The anesthesiologist needs to do a proper job of explaining what is going to happen in your brain over the next few days. He talks about the potential physical effects, such as nausea, drowsiness, or sleeplessness, but he does not tell you your brain may function differently and be weird for a few days. Anesthesia puts you to sleep, but this is not normal sleep.

This chemical sleep bathes the cells in your brain so they are pickled in something new and different. After surgery, this "pickling juice" must be washed out of your brain. No one prepares you for this transition. The IV in your arm is part of this flushing mechanism. Drinking lots of water is an integral part of this flushing system, and that plastic breathing thing you struggle to suck out of is a part of this too.

I did not do much sleeping after surgery. Again, some of the information you should know is sleep changes with these chemicals trying to run out of your brain. But when I did close my eyes, the show was weird. I know I store information in pictures – that has always been my preferred processing format. Ask me if I know someone, and their picture pops into my brain. So, with these chemicals activating my brain, the photos of others were wild. I went through a movie screen roll of 38mm film of every person I have ever encountered.

Try to sleep and the pictures just kept rolling. Saw my third-grade teacher and remembered she raised a hen in a cage in the middle of the room all year: "Biddy Hen". I have no idea of the teacher's name, but a great pic.

When I taught college, I made a solid effort to learn every student's name on day one. I went around the room and asked everyone to say their name and tell one important or unusual thing about themselves. I could picture them and use the details to grab their first name. I required them to stay in the same seat all semester. Rolls and rolls of those students went through my head.

We encode data in three main ways: images, sounds, and motion. The first two are easy to understand. The third is something like this: you move through space, and let us say you are walking someplace, and your brain records the action, or you are learning to swing a bat, and your brain must focus on the motion and nothing else to make you a good batter. We each have preferences for the storage of information. As I have said, mine is picture storage. Did you know that emails can be stored as images?

Recovering from anesthesia, I close my eyes, and a white circle appears filled with fast-moving images of emails. Come on! Who knew?

REFLECTING

1. If you could access the database in your brain, what would you be looking to re-experience and why?
2. What would you want to erase and why?

SECTION 10

EVALUATION – A BONUS ESSAY!

LOOKING IN THE MIRROR

How many mirrors do you have in the house? Where are they? How do they function for you and your family? Did you know that the earliest mirrors date back 8,000 years? They were found in Turkey and were made of obsidian, a volcanic glass. They were also remarkably good at producing an image. When we see ourselves in a mirror, we can have a variety of responses. I look pretty. I am good-looking for my age. Or, oh no, that bump will erupt as a pimple!

Mirrors allow us to see ourselves as others see us. Rarely do we have the opportunity to step outside ourselves and carefully look at what others see. Taking stock of how we look, who we are, and how we come across to others is essential. Yet, we are rarely allowed to do this. Most of the time, we are busy living and engaging in our lives with only glances at the mirror of life.

I have a friend who told me of an exciting way to take stock. She has a particular journal. I know several people who have kept journals and have stacks of them in the back of their closet which date back to early adolescence. That is the time people begin to keep a journal. As we move into puberty, we become more aware of ourselves. Significant changes are taking place physically, emotionally, and intellectually. Journals are a perfect place to meet yourself. For those who have kept journals, there generally comes a time when old journals are reviewed. Often, this brings a sense of appreciation for the past and maybe some laughs.

My friend who journals has a unique process. Each day, she writes one line in her journal. As the years progressed, she used the same journal and wrote one line on the page for each day. This accumulation of one-liners is fascinating as these one-liners march down the page year after year. A quick comparison from one year to the next is revealing. I am intrigued when I think about the possibility of comparing a day at a time over a year.

How have I changed over time? I know my looks are different, and I do not need a volcanic glass to clarify that. At the same time, I have not thought about how my thinking might change or my focus might shift. This would be fascinating. I must pick the right book to use. And then the right pen. I may find a fancy fountain pen for the particular journal and a leather-bound book with blank pages. Or I could get my Bic pen and the spiral notebook in the desk drawer. Regardless of the hardware I choose, the process is the critical part. I write one line daily, and those reflections are bound to be valuable.

REFLECTING

NOW THAT YOU HAVE SPENT A YEAR REFLECTING, FILL THE PAGE WITH WHAT YOU HAVE LEARNED.

Comments from Readers

D. Krawczyk, Youth Leader
Gloria is a down-to-earth, inspiring educator and counselor who puts her heart into her work. Her blog is relatable and thought-provoking, positively, and constructively! I look forward to more!

M. Francis
I love how Gloria's blog entries help us find our place at any moment. She makes us think, and even more importantly, she inspires us to be the best versions of ourselves!

M. Smith
Gloria's words inspire me on so many levels. She develops positive relationships with children, youth, and adults! Now, her written word leaves me thinking about how to discover more about myself and how I can improve!

K. Lindstedt
Gloria's blogs are insightful, thought-provoking, and positive. She has a mastery of language, examining a common expression, word, or emotion and relating it to everyday life. I always feel uplifted and a little wiser after reading her words. I highly recommend this book.

J. Fox, Retired Minister
It is easy to relate to. Stories make me smile. Thoughtful questions. Insightful stories. It is an excellent companion for pushing my mind forward or directing me to think reflectively and creatively.

E. F. Kandell, Esq., Professional certified mediator
Every high school and college student should read Dr. Vanderhorst's book and think and write in response to her prompts following each essay. Each short essay starts with an easy and practical situation that all humans face during their lives. Your Mental Storage Locker, for instance, begins by talking about the physical clutter and junk we accumulate and then pivots to encourage the examination of trauma and early memories. All the essays use excellent analogies that prompt deeper exploration.

This book is akin to mental dental floss!

Your Next Chapter Starts Here

If you enjoyed this book, then we have a perfect next step into deeper self-discovery.

The Life Inventory Assessment™ is the ultimate tool to reflect on your life and uncover opportunities for growth and clarity.

Unlock the wisdom within you by visiting

https://bit.ly/readreflectrespond

or scan the QR code below.